FINDING PLACE

A Holy Journey of Chinese Adoption

By Lars & Katie Stromberg

Dedicated to an unknown Chinese Mother.

You are so loved.

FOREWARD

In 2014, my wife Katie and I adopted our daughter, Lydia, from China. This book is the story of that process, told from both my perspective in the years following—with the benefit of hindsight and reflection—and also from Katie's perspective as it was happening in the form of blog entry. I feel honored that you would join us for this journey as we tell this story that continues to unfold.

But why write this book, and more importantly, why should you read it? Well, as with any work of art worth consuming, this is first and foremost for Katie and me and our family. It's a work of posterity, a memoir for Lydia to have forever, and words that were in both of us that needed to come out. If we were the only ones who ever read and reflected on these words, they would be well worth writing.

But you have decided to read them as well. It's our hope and prayer that this will be an encouraging story of God's faithfulness, that it will warm your heart and resonate on some deep level. We pray that you might come away with a new understanding of the character of God who calls us his children. We pray that you might cry some, laugh some, lament some, rejoice some.

We also hope that some of you, or even just one of you, might read this book and feel a call to adopt a child as well.

We wrote this book primarily because it is the book we wish we had when we were beginning our adoption journey. We needed information on the international adoption process, but more so we needed to understand the emotional realities of the adoption process. We hope that others who are considering adoption get a full view of the process and are nothing but encouraged to say yes to this call.

Becoming adoptive parents has been the great adventure of our lifetime and we're honored to have you join us through this book. Because we believe so firmly that adoption is near to the heart of God, a percentage of all proceeds from book sales will go to fund others who have said yes to adoption and are in need of encouragement in their journey. Know that by simply picking up this book, you are part of something very near to the heart of God.

As you read this story, you may sense God nudging you in some way. If you would like to connect with us to talk about adoption or anything else that God is doing in your heart, please email me at larsericstromberg@gmail.com.

Thank you for journeying with us.

CHAPTER 1

BROKENESS

Every story of God and his people begins in the same place: human brokenness and need for a Savior. As a pastor, I know this. I know it from the reverberating echoes of God's great story in Scripture. I know it in my own life. I know it in the lives of those I minister to daily. I know the truth that seems so very contradictory to everything I learned in church, that the gospel is indeed, as Frederick Buechner puts it, "bad news before it is good news." We cannot be made whole without first being broken.

And so here, like all the other stories of God's faithfulness, our story begins.

When Katie and I were nineteen years old, about nine months into our relationship, we began to talk modestly about marriage, our expectations, our hopes and dreams. I shared two dreams with her. First, I shared that I want to be a pastor of a dying rural church (not exactly the sales pitch I would suggest for any young men who are reading this). Second, I shared that I would like to have three or four children. Being from a family of four, I was always intrigued by the dynamics within larger families. I wanted to be part of the "Brady Bunch," but without Jan or Sam the butcher. Katie only shared one thing: "Lars, if we're going to go any further, you have to know that I plan on adopting a girl from China. You'll have to get on board with that."

Looking back, it's amazing that neither of us scared the other away but remained with one another in a beautifully simple way. Life moved quickly through engagement, marriage, and seminary. I never became a rural pastor—that call changed swiftly. Instead I took my first call as a youth pastor in the Chicago suburbs. At the same time we welcomed our first child into the world, our dear Quinten, a beautiful boy with a shock of bright red hair like his father. Before long we were learning how to do ministry, moving into the church parsonage, and welcoming another little one, an attentive and joyful boy named Albin. Life was good. Our boys were growing to be best friends, ministry thrived, life moved on.

Then we began to try for our third child, the red-haired daughter that Katie and I desperately wanted. That's when we came face to face with the brokenness of human life. We had experienced a painful miscarriage before bringing Quinn into the world, but that seemed like a distant memory after two healthy pregnancies—brokenness that was so quickly redeemed. So when we miscarried in late 2010 it was a shock. We had been foolish enough to think that we could perfectly plan our next child's arrival, that we could closely estimate the month of birth, year in school, and age difference to the boys. I remember holding Katie's hand as she laid on the gurney, ready to have her DNC completed. As I prayed for her, for us, I felt a deep guilt for trying to control the process. I wasn't mad at God. I don't have that in me. I just realized that we hadn't effectively given the process over to him.

And that's what we did. We prayed earnestly, humbled our hearts, and gave control over to God. So when the second miscarriage came five months later, we felt a bit paralyzed. There was a sneaking suspicion that maybe God was trying to tell us something. Was there a deep sin that we were being punished for? Was God protecting us from something? We felt clearly that we need to slow things down, release the pressure to get pregnant, focus on our boys, and heal from the stinging loss of two failed pregnancies.

In the fall of 2011, after an excellent summer of fun and family together, we decided to try again for a little one. This time, we told our parents and friends, and put out an "all call" to the prayer warriors in our lives. We felt a new lease to be excited about adding to our family. But we had trouble conceiving, which was completely new to us. In those months, tears came readily and odd times—on a phone call with parents, watching our boys act like boys instead of babies. I even remember that the one time that year I had the opportunity to sit with my wife during our worship service, we were singing "He's Got the Whole World in His Hands." When we sang the line "He's got the itty-bitty babies in his hands," we both lost it. Katie was squeezing my hand harder than anyone reasonably should.

We were cautiously excited to receive a positive pregnancy test in February 2012. Katie was certainly not herself. There was little joy because of the fear of loss looming. I knew she wouldn't have any attachment to this pregnancy until she heard a heartbeat. At nine weeks we went to get an ultrasound from our midwives. Shaking and scared, we heard a heartbeat and gloriously exhaled. We felt God's blessing, the presence of answered prayer, and we could see the end of a painful journey in the distance.

In early April, we went in for our twelve-week ultrasound, and within minutes we knew that something was wrong. As our doctor searched feverishly for a heartbeat, seconds felt like hours and Katie began to shake her head and tear up. We heard our doctor say plainly, "There is just nothing there. I'm so sorry." Then something remarkable happened. Katie grabbed our doctor with one hand and me with the other and began to pray. It was a visceral, guttural lament. I couldn't possibly tell you the words she used—my shock kept me from cataloging them. But I know she wasn't pleading for the life of this child or shaking her fist at God. She was praying for herself, for her heart, for our family, for hope.

Two days later, Katie was once again getting prepped for a DNC surgery. I spoke my love and pride for her, for her strength and her heart. She asked simply, "What do you think this all means? Am I just done having kids."

My response was simple, "Let's give your body a rest. We can talk about that later."

I sent her into surgery and sat in the waiting room and began writing a sermon. It was Holy Week, and I was scheduled to preach for the Good Friday service the next day. My colleague lovingly offered to preach on my behalf, but I had a strong sense that I wanted to meet the brokenness of my life head on.

This is the transcript of that sermon:

I remember distinctly a Bible study leader challenging me during Holy Week. His name was Jeremy, a college-aged student who had agreed to disciple a group of high school boys through Bible study. He was a passionate, cool guy that any junior higher would look up to. "Ok boys, how many of you are wearing crosses?" Of the six of us, three had crosses somewhere—I was wearing mine on a simple necklace. "Why do we wear those, guys? If this week teaches us anything, it's that Christ defeated the cross. This is symbol of death and pain and sorrow. I think we need a symbol for the empty tomb, because that is really what we are all about. We're not about death, we're about life." I was fired up by this. I put my cross back in my dresser drawer and became passionate about the resurrection.

This was a good word for me to hear as a fifteen-year-old. Really this human existence boils down to this: "Death is the mortal problem. Life is the immortal answer." If it came down to it, I was choosing to identify with life and shunning symbols of death. Who really wants to talk about a cross anyway?

Many Christians have followed a similar path. There are a great number of Good Friday preachers this evening in churches all over the country and the world who are preaching the same sermon. Allow me to spoil it for you: "Christ went to the cross for your sins, but he didn't stay there. Because for every Friday, there is Sunday. Death is not the final answer. The cross holds no power. Now let's rise and sing 'Up from the Grave.'" I'd be a fraud to say that I'm any different. The smallest part of me is clinging to the hope that Easter Sunday is coming, and I know it to be true. But it's Friday tonight. As much as I'd love to look forward, I feel strongly that we are meant to stay here—at the cross—this evening.

I can speak this evening in the same tenor as the apostle Paul did to the church in Corinth in 1 Corinthians 2:1-5:

> In the same way, my brothers and sisters, when I came to proclaim to you God's secret purpose, I did not come equipped with any brilliance of speech or intellect. You may as well know now that it was my secret determination to concentrate entirely on Jesus Christ and the fact of his death upon the cross. As a matter of fact, in myself I was feeling far from strong; I was nervous and rather shaky. What I said and preached had none of the attractiveness of the clever mind, but it was a demonstration of the power of the Spirit! Plainly God's purpose was that your faith should not rest upon man's cleverness but upon the power of God.

Some of you know why I am far from strong—why I'm nervous and rather shaky—tonight. Katie and I have been through a nearly two-year period of loss, having lost our third pregnancy in that time this week. This church has been so wonderfully supportive, but this experience has highlighted a movement in heart and mind that God has been shaping for a couple years. I care for a lot of people in times of pain, death, and great need, and I often struggle for words. I find myself in critical moments where a comforting word needs to be spoken, and I may say something like, "Well, we don't know what God has in all of this, but there is something better at the end of this. God has a great plan." Are these words true? Yes. God is in this—he has better things ahead, a great plan. But do you see what I've done? I've bypassed Good Friday for the sake of Easter. I've stuffed the cross in the dresser drawer. I've adopted a theology of glory, a belief that says that God is a winner, that he exists primarily to make us feel better about ourselves, that his presence with us means more blessings than difficulties, and that the closer we cling to him the better he will make our lives.

The problem is, despite how well we follow Jesus, we often are not winners. People lose jobs. Marriages fall apart. Children disappoint their parents. Parents disappoint their children. Cancer strikes. People die. Little lives have hearts that just stop beating. We can ignore these realities, gloss them over, combat them with positive sentiment, but when they strike, they bring the crushing reality of loss with them. The assurance that everything works out with God is pretty unstable when facing the excruciating reality of death and loss. Yet we crave life over death, so we all too often stuff the cross in the drawer and speak of life.

Well, I can't afford to do that tonight, and I don't think you can either. I think we need to replace a theology of glory with a theology of the cross. Instead of saying, "God is going to pull me through this," we need to be able to say,

"God is here with me." If I flee from the reality of broken-ness and loss, then I may well be fleeing his presence be-cause this is where Christ went. He went to loss and death and separation on the cross. And he didn't do this for himself—he did it for you and me. I thank Jesus that he didn't gloss over the cross, that he didn't try to escape death! Instead he went further in and faced it.

Our whole family has been so sad as we have come face to face with the cross this week yet again. As I'm sure you have done at times, I began to ask why: Why us? Why this again?

I was taking the garbage out to the dumpster under a full moon and asking God to say something in the midst of the pain. I started to say, "I'm sorry Lord, if this is due to something that I have done or something I've failed to do . . . " And then I remembered Jesus's words in John 14 to the disciples mere hours before he was arrested. Fac-ing the cross, he told them, "I will not leave you orphaned or abandoned," and I realized that it doesn't mean every-thing is going to be okay. It means that Jesus is with us acutely in all the ways that life is not okay. And I said a prayer out loud in the parking lot, which I hope didn't scare anyone. I said, "Jesus, I'm sorry that you have to go through this with me." What may seem like a strange prayer is to me the core of a theology of the cross. It's not about God's great plan to bring me out of this and make it all better. It's about God's great plan to never leave me orphaned or abandoned, to go to death so that he could be with me in that death.

When the apostle Paul is at a place of weakness, he has a choice to speak solely of the resurrection, but instead he says, "You may as well know now that it was my secret determination to concentrate entirely on Jesus Christ and the fact of his death upon the cross." I'm a fraud to stand before you and assume that I have any eloquence or brilliance of intellect. I'm not very strong myself at all. But I can point you to the cross and trust that the Spirit will speak to your spirit as you ponder this wonderful symbol. An object of death and torture where our Lord chooses to tabernacle, to dwell with us.

Last week, I met with a church member who was dealing with a cross in his life that was unimaginably difficult. His life was crashing down all around him, and with tears in his eyes he said, "You know what though, as hard as it's all been, I'm seeing crosses everywhere that I look. In every tree, in each angle of every house, the cross is there." I was able to say, "That's a reminder that Christ is there."

Jesus chooses the cross, and we ought to choose to see him there as well. We cannot find the solution of Easter life until we lay at the feet of the cross and ponder the problem of death. The pain and death we've gone through is the problem with the world. And that is where Christ chooses to meet us. Don't gloss over the cross. Don't stuff it away. Don't deny it of its power. Hear the call to come to the cross and die because this is where we may well find the true assurance of life.

I preached through tears with my wife sitting in the second pew on the right. We worshiped and tried to trust, wondering what God would do with this story of brokenness that was looking more broken with each new day. We prayed earnestly for hope on that Friday night.

Four days later, a girl named Wu DanQing was born in the Henan province of China to a mother who faced an impossible decision. We had no idea that two stories of brokenness were coming together.

CHAPTER 2

DECISIONS

O nce the dust had settled after Easter, we were exhausted—Katie in body, both of us in spirit. We spent a few days in quiet. I'm quite sure that there was plenty of noise—two young boys running about the house, friends checking in on us, people dropping off meals, work to be done—but it was distinctly quiet because we weren't talking about the only thing that really mattered: *What does this loss and brokenness mean for us?*

I think we both knew that it was decision time. We had to decide whether we could ever try for a child again, or if it was too painful. It's no wonder that we avoided that conversation. We had never had to make a decision like this.

Decision making is a tricky thing. As Sophocles said, "Quick decisions are unsafe decisions." I think that there is a spectrum of decision-making attributes, and like most spectrums the polar ends are the least desirable. On one end, you have those who are paralyzed by the reality of decisions—the agonizers, the over-thinkers, the analysis junkies, the easily overwhelmed. On the other end of the spectrum are the overly decisive types—the unbudging, the preprocessors, the systematists, the cholerics, the don't-question-me-I've-made-up-my-mind types. We all have natures that place us somewhere on this spectrum, and the way we make decisions says a lot about the quality and content of our lives.

Well, some may view me as a decisive person but they are only partially correct. When it comes to making decisions on my own, I'm rather decisive. I suppose I never placed a huge value on making the absolutely right choice, so I just make a choice and deal with it. I don't agonize but I also don't care about being right. When my mom would take me shopping for school, I would grab a pair of pants off the rack and tell her that I didn't need to try them on, that I was sure they would work just fine. When I had to decide on which college I would go to, I found the first college that I liked and ripped up the applications for every other school without looking back. When I decided that I wanted to marry Katie, I had no existential torment. The decision was easy and I haven't second-guessed it. Even today, when I order my breakfast, I find the first thing on the menu that looks good, and I just simply enjoy it. I eat my Denver omelet, and I never ponder the virtues of the waffle being eaten by the guy in the booth next to me. This is how I decide. Maybe it's a deficiency. Maybe it's God's grace for me. Either way, personal decisions have tended to be easy for me.

But when decisions are made with others, I swing to the other end of the spectrum. I am a peacemaker at heart, which can cause me to be indecisive and deferential to others. This decision was far beyond me. It was a negotiation that, at best, would be a joint decision that Katie and I felt equally good about and, at worst, would be a stalemate where someone would get hurt. And if I'm being honest, I really can't carry the weight in this kind of decision. I often hear men say, "My wife and I are pregnant," or "My wife and I are expecting," which is, technically or otherwise, completely untrue. The man's role in this pregnancy is really one of support. We don't experience it bodily. We aren't awakened by sickness or kicking or heartburn. For me, our pregnancies only became totally real when we were packing a bag to head to hospital. So, knowing that Katie's stake in this decision outweighed my own, I intended to let her speak first.

One night that week, lying in bed, I began, "Honey, when do you want to talk about our next steps here? I don't want to rush you, but I know we need to come up with a plan for the immediate future, for the sake of our sanity."

"I know", she replied. "Lars, just tell me, are we just done? Is our family complete?"

The question hung out there for ten seconds. This was

not as I planned. This was not a pair of pants. This was not a Denver omelet. This was the future of our family. I needed to be on one end of the decisiveness scale or the other here. Strong and firm, or cautious and careful. I couldn't be me because my decision-making process wasn't going to work here.

So I went off script and out of character and in that moment—a true pivot point in my life—I decided to say what I knew to be true as decisively as possible. Breaking the silence, I said, "No, we're not done, but I think your body is done for a while, maybe forever. There is no joy in thinking about trying again, and I just think your body and heart need a rest. But we're not done."

Katie nodded, looking at me reassuringly as if to say that those were the words she needed to hear, and that was the decisive manner that she needed to hear them in. Maybe Katie was even a little attracted to this new side of me—to this man who was decisive rather than one who took the typical diplomatic approach of "well, whatever you think honey. I'm supportive." I felt good. I felt assertive. I felt like a good husband.

After a bit of thought, Katie said, "Well maybe we should look into adoption again." I had a sense deep down that our conversation might land here, but it's hard to overstate how ridiculous and illogical it was for us to seriously think about adoption. And yet, the decision had been made that we weren't done as a family, and this was *the* path forward. That dude Sophocles was right. Quick decisions are unsafe decisions, and this decision was anything but safe.

■

Wu DanQing was born with a cleft palate, which means that the roof of her mouth was wide open to her nasal cavity. Other than this detail, we don't definitively know our daughter's story. Since 1978, China has held a one-child policy in the interest of population control. Though there have always been exceptions for certain ethnic minorities and the wealthy who are willing to pay the fines associated with additional children, the vast majority of Chinese families had to abide by this policy, either because of financial constraints or concerns about legal and penal repercussions. This policy put newborn girls and the disabled at high risk, with the seminal importance of household economics and a strong male cultural preference. In short, girls couldn't earn enough money to eventually take care of their aging parents, and disabled children could not be fully helpful to the family system. Since you only got one shot at a child, a strong, healthy male was certainly preferable. Over fifty thousand Chinese children, most of them girls, have been adopted by US parents alone since Chinese adoption opened in 1992. For every one of these precious children who found forever families, there are uncountable children who died in orphanages, were trafficked into the streets, or were simply killed in infancy. It's sobering, and far worse than I could ever investigate or write about.

For some of us, quick, and ultimately unsafe, decisions are of our own choosing. For others there is no other option. Think about the decision so many mothers have had to make: You've given birth to a girl, your family system is dirt poor, your husband is severely disappointed that it's not a boy, and none of your neighbors can know or else they could report you to the authorities. You have no way of legally giving up your child for adoption. If you bring your child to a hospital or police station you could be thrown in jail or forced to face stiff fines. So there are only three options: Find a rich family member who will covertly assume them as their own and pay the fines; let the newborn child die and pretend like they were never there for the rest of your life; or abandon your child in such a way that they have a chance of finding a way to a hospital or orphanage. The first option is rare, especially for a huge segment of Chinese people who live in poor agrarian rural areas. The second option happens all too often, countless times that were never recorded. Thank God for the third option.

It's for these reasons that we aren't likely to ever know our daughter's story. But here is what I *chose* to believe. I believe that because of her cleft palate, Wu DanQing couldn't suck from her mother's breast, as she was unable to create the suction, and the life-giving milk came out of her nose instead. I believe her mother cared for her for a few days and realized that she was not going to be able to nurse, and that if she didn't do something her daughter would die. I believe that surgery or hospital bills were not financially possible for her. I believe that she and the father of her child decided that the third option was the only option. I believe that they loved their daughter. I believe that this decision was motivated by love and a desire to save her daughter's life. I can never know this for sure, but in my heart, I believe this story to be true.

What we do know is that a beautiful girl was placed on the steps of an orphanage by the Bao Si Bridge in the city of Xinyang in the Henan province in the dark, early morning hours of April 16, 2012. She was discovered by a police officer and then brought back to the Xinyang Children's Welfare Institute, where she was determined to be about six days old. Her picture was posted on a bulletin board outside the orphanage and in the local paper, standard procedure after an abandonment. She went unclaimed and became an official resident of Xinyang orphanage, where she was given the name Wu DanQing. *Wu* is a common surname, and *DanQing* is a word that depicts the common palette of traditional Chinese painting, primarily red and bluish green.

I believe that somewhere—in a parked car or a nearby bus stop—a courageous mother, who just had made a quick, gut-wrenching, and extremely unsafe decision, watched as her daughter was scooped up out of the smoggy cold and brought inside. I believe she knew that she would never see her child again, but I also believe that a God she likely couldn't name gave her a sense of peace and calm, honoring the bold and loving decision she was forced to make. I believe that God wept along with her at that moment.

CHAPTER 3

PROVISIONS

When I took my first pastoral call (read here, first real job), we were twenty-five years old. My church (which as of 2020 I am still joyfully serving) wrote a stipulation into my job description that I needed to live within five miles of church. Katie and I decided to take out a pen and draw a five-mile circle around Hinsdale, Illinois, to see what our options were. There were a few prerequisites: (a) it needed to be on or near a train line. Katie had grown up in nearby Wheaton and had a fair amount of nostalgia around Chicago suburban towns along the train line, plus I needed to be able to take the train to work being that we were a one car family; (b) it needed to be within our modest price range; and (c) it needed to make us feel like adults, because we were unequivocally adults, and even though we *certainly*

didn't need to own a home to prove that we were adults, still . . .

We immediately realized that our options within the five-mile circle were mostly near its margins. My church is located in a very affluent area of the western suburbs of Chicago, and we found that nearly every place we could possibly afford was four and a half to five miles away. We eventually settled on a small condo that was 4.8 miles from church, along the train line and with one parking spot. We called up a financial advisor before signing the papers and he very clearly stated that no matter how he crunched the numbers, we were on the edge of whether we should be buying or not. His advice was that we ask the church for more money or to extend our range to seven or eight miles away.

But remember, we were adults. We had rented for the duration of the seminary years, but I had a real job now. I didn't want to ask for more money. Heck, I was just happy to have a job. No, we'd make it work. Rice and beans for dinner. Walking instead of driving. We'd make it work. So, for the very first time, we signed on the dotted line about a thousand times, and someone handed us some keys, and we owned a home.

In late September we moved our possessions out of our spacious Chicago apartment that went on forever and had a dining room that was twice the size of any room in our new condo, and we crammed our stuff into that small condo that so represented our adulthood. My mom came down from

Minnesota to help us make our new condo a home. We moved in on a Friday. On Saturday we had a "100-year rain" which appeared to be completely centered on our small condo complex, and much of that rain ended up in our basement where the bulk of our boxes were. I'll never forget watching the panes of our window well shattering and my mom capturing the huge wall of water in a mop bucket and asking, "What am I doing? I have nowhere to bail this. I'm in a basement."

This should have perhaps been an indication that all was not well. I'm not a huge believer in the retributive justice of God. I don't think that he would look at the misguided, if not well intentioned, decision of two twenty-five-year-olds and then decide to send a storm upon us. That said, I can't deny that I had my questions at this point. Within thirty-six hours of moving in I was already sensing that we might have made a huge mistake.

Within six months, I *knew* we had made a mistake. We simply were not making it. We had flooding two more times. We were going into credit card debt in order to make our mortgage payments. I was constantly cutting ministry opportunities short so that I could catch a train. And we could smell the cigarette smoke from our neighbors' apartment every time we walked down the stairs. I had to go to my church, tail between my legs, and admit that we simply weren't making it in our condo. God graciously provided us a parsonage option right next to church, where we still live today. A year after signing on the dotted line we were packing up boxes and putting our condo up on the market. The only issue was that we were putting our condo on the market in late 2007, which will always be remembered as the absolutely worst time since the Great Depression to try and sell a home. As we moved into the little white house next door to church, our condo adventure was far from over.

Over the next eight years, I would serve as the world's worst landlord for a property that I desperately wanted to sell or 'accidentally' light on fire. A few highlights from this grand time of life: Spending countless hours with a city worker named Donovan as he explained to me the intricacies of how tree roots clog pipes while trying to pick the world's largest chunk of lettuce out of his teeth. Fixing a drip in the kitchen sink while listening to Arcade Fire super loud and occasionally uttering mild swears while not realizing that our tenants' grandma was sleeping on the couch about eight feet away the entire time. Spilling Drano on one of my tenant's vintage Japanese comic books and putting it back on the shelf hoping that the chemicals wouldn't burn a hole through his bookshelf. Listening to my wife scream over the telephone that she had to throw away a dead rat that was "the size of a small dog." Conversing in the parking lot with my eighty-one-year-old tenant who told me that if I didn't give him his deposit back, he would curse the apartment forever while poking me with a rolled-up newspaper. Having a bird fly at mach speed into the back of my head while I trimmed the front bushes. Patching walls, installing light fixtures, replacing hot-water heaters, and praying in the power of the Spirit for the health of the forty-year-old furnace that was severely rusted and held together with duct tape in at least two places.

Sure, laugh. Enjoy yourself. But this place was an albatross around our family's neck. We had the house on the market three times without any movement at all before pulling back and taking on another tenant. We prayed earnestly for eight years that God would help us sell this place, that God would lift this burden from us. But he didn't. God moves in a mysterious way.

■

When we decided in 2012 to officially explore Chinese adoption, there were so many roadblocks that it seems silly to even try to name them all. Since that day in the sophomore townhouses at college when Katie told me, "Lars, if we're going to move forward in this relationship, you have to know that I plan on adopting a little girl from China someday." I knew that Chinese adoption was a distinct possibility, but we had hardly talked about it for a decade. We were in the thick of raising our two boys, and there were so many restrictions on Chinese adoption that talking about it was just a waste of words.

For one thing, you had to have a minimum combined age of sixty-one as a couple to even begin paperwork. Additionally, you had to meet specific financial qualifications to even be considered, and you had to have a medical history that was devoid of cancer, depression, and numerous congenital diseases or genetic maladies. The checklist to simply begin the process was so overwhelming that we didn't even seriously think about it for nine years of marriage. But now that this was getting real, we began to face the checklist boldly.

The craziest thing happened: that which seemed so overwhelming and impossible became possible, yea even mildly encouraging. We realized that we had just surpassed the age requirement. We're blessed with an incredibly clean bill of health and few genetic deficits, so much so that we've had doctors go through their rap sheet and say, "Seriously? Nothing?" The kicker was the financial requirements. I had just received a ten-thousand-dollar raise in January, something that I never expected. (If you don't believe me, I dare you buy your local pastor a cup of coffee and ask him or her if they have ever received a ten-thousand-dollar raise or expect to receive one. Be sure to cover your eyes so that you don't get sprayed with scalding hot coffee.) That unthinkable pay bump notched us narrowly above the gross income requirements for Chinese adoptions. Things seemed to be coming together.

However, there was the issue of net worth. At the end of the checklist was a complicated worksheet to calculate our net worth as a family. I began to read it and my heart sank. The minimum requirements for net worth were over half again the total of my salary. And short of my salary, we had no assets, only debts. School loan debt, credit card debt, debts to church for a down payment, car debt, and of course the notorious condo that we were totally underwater on, figuratively and occasionally literally. The largest physical asset I could think of was my guitar, valued at a paltry fourteen-hundred dollars. I had all but resigned myself to the fact that I'd have to face my wife and say something along the lines of "We can't adopt because God called me to be a pastor and so it's probably his fault." I called our adoption agency, Chinese Children Adoption International (CCAI), as a last-ditch effort to see if there was any way around the fact that we had little money and no assets. The woman I spoke to continued to ask about the condo, and I explained the whole story, from biblical floods to mammoth rats to Drano spills. She said, "Well, as China sees it, that condo is an asset." I wrote the original purchase price on the worksheet (call it laziness but I had not had it officially appraised since we purchased it in 2006) and punched the numbers into my calculator about ten times to make sure I wasn't seeing things. Our net worth cleared the modest floor by a couple hundred dollars.

And there it was. Nine years of wondering. Nine years of prayers and tears and my self-esteem being punctured by the fact that I couldn't even fake being a capable landlord. Nine years of asking, "God why in the world are you allowing this place to weigh us down emotionally, spiritually, financially, and psychologically with no apparent desire to lift us out?" And it became clear: this condo was all about something we never could have seen. Truly, God is his own interpreter, and sometimes he provides in ways that boggle the mind and humble the proudest heart.

A year after bringing our daughter home we finally felt permission to take a bath on our condo and sell it for whatever we could get for it. We ultimately took a seventy-thousand-dollar loss just to remove the title of landlord and start fresh. Even as we prepared for the closing God was still surprising us. Katie wrote this email to our family:

> Last night at 5:35, after all our papers were signed for our closing earlier that day and right before our Gotcha Day party for Liddy, we got a call... From our lawyer saying "I'm so sorry but I had the numbers wrong, you need another $1000 for the closing." Sheesh!!! (We were already maxed at what we needed to bring to closing, over $24,000) And I knew this would mean we couldn't pay our bills the rest of the month... We went on with the party, which was totally wonderful! At the end of the night,

we opened cards. A friend who used to live in China, had set out little Chinese red envelopes, and people had left money gifts in them, a Chinese custom for special events. We opened the envelopes to find, $695! Earlier that day some other friends from church had gifted us $300. $995 in total. When we went to deposit the money Lars found another $20, which put us at $1015. What? Crazy!?! We could write a book, on the crazy creative ways God provides.

As we signed the papers over to a new owner, and as we handed the real estate lawyer a twenty-four-thousand-dollar personal check to cover the difference, my daughter was bouncing on my knee, and I simply had to laugh. I will never again question whether God is powerful, providential, or caring.

CHAPTER 4

WIDENING THE CIRCLE

By most accounts, mainstream Western society is at its most woefully isolated right now. When was the last time your neighbor rang your doorbell and then came in with no agenda other than to connect? When was the last time you visited a neighbor to simply ask for an egg, sugar, or flour? Heck, when was the last time you had an actual conversation on your phone? Sure, in many ways we are more connected than we have ever been in human history, but I could just as easily make the case that we have never been more disconnected. The byproduct of this uber-connected disconnect is that we don't really know each other as well as we think we do, and when we ourselves come to a point where we desperately need to be known, we don't know where to turn or who to trust.

In my years of pastoral counseling, one common thread I've observed is the preponderance of lonely and isolated people, many of whom are very personable and run in robust social circles. How many couples don't *really* talk with one another? How many leaders get in trouble in their workplace because they don't have anyone to rein them in? How many people are surrounded by people and yet experience the most intense forms of loneliness? How many well-meaning people don't know that they are deathly afraid of emotional intimacy? We naturally drift away from the people that we most need. It's our sinful and broken nature pulling us away from the life-source for which we are so thirsty.

My word to these dear people who come to me has been the same over and over again: *widen the circle*. Your marriage is falling apart? Widen the circle of who knows and who is praying. Your child is trapped in addiction? Widen the circle of people who can care for you. You are suffering with depression or anxiety? Widen the circle of friends and you'll find that you're not alone.

Widen the circle. It's an easy phrase to say and remember but hard to actually live into. Once we received our adoption approval we were forced to practice these words that I had spoken to so many. It was time to widen the circle in a number of ways. We needed prayer partners for the journey. We needed other adoptive parents to share their wisdom. We needed the emotional support of our friends, family, and church. We needed financial support to the tune of thirty-thousand dollars in order to be able to adopt. The default mechanism is to isolate, not put yourself out there. But we had no choice but to fight against this tendency. If we didn't widen the circle, there was no way to make this adoption a reality.

The problem with widening the circle is not a social one. It's an intensely emotional one. When we get to the point where we need to widen the circle, we experience pain because we are at the end of our means, our resources, our selves. We were faced with our neediness—and that was painful enough—but then we had to verbalize that neediness to others in our own words, which can be excruciating. But here's the thing: it's only excruciating in our minds. It's not actually excruciating. If those with whom we widen the circle are not just utilitarian objects for us, if they are real people that we care about, then this actually isn't painful. When others come to me with their neediness, I'm not embarrassed, not judgmental, not piteous. I respect them *more* and often feel a privileged intimacy in knowing them better. The pain we associate with widening the circle is nothing more than a deception from some deep dark place. Being known, being at the end of ourselves, ought to be life giving and painless.

We had to widen the circle in our adoption, and it was

painful initially until we realized that it really wasn't. Our biggest need was financial. We made as many adjustments as we could, eating out minimally and tucking away whatever money we could, but we were well aware that we needed to come up with thirty-thousand dollars that we didn't have. It's hard for me to ask for money. I work in a strange profession where everyone knows exactly what I make and we take a collection every week to make sure that the staff gets paid. It's awkward for me to ask for money when people are already giving on a regular basis. So when people asked, "How can we help with the adoption?" the last thing I wanted to say was "financial help would be good, and this time directly to us, please." But we needed the help, so we got creative. We opened a profile on Adopt-Together, a crowdfunding platform focused on adoptive families. We sent out support letters sharing our needs with family and close friends. We sent the link to our profile out to anyone who would ask us how they could help. We agreed to let a friend organize a rummage sale at church which became an entire weekend with a gym packed to the rafters with beautiful stuff and a cadre of hilarious stories, like the octogenarian who purchased a pristine 1989 Nintendo Gameboy with ten games. When I asked her, "Is this for your grandkids?" she said, "No. I don't have grandkids." Or the guy who came in the last hour of the sale and purchased four tube TVs that had an average weight of about 150 pounds. I asked him if he was purchasing these to sell the parts. He replied, "No. I just thought that my dad would love to have these in his basement." I laughed. He gave no evidence that he was joking. Or the church member who dropped off seven empty propane tanks as a donation. I didn't have the heart to tell her that I couldn't sell those and that she might have been confused about how propane tanks worked.

Looking back on it now, widening the circle was the most life giving and miraculous part of the adoption process in many ways. By sharing the link to our AdoptTogether profile and working hard at the rummage sale, we saw people come out of the woodwork, people that we didn't even know were part of the circles that we were seeking to widen. Within hours of going live on AdoptTogether we had received a hundred dollars from a couple we went to college with but hadn't spoken to since then. A high-school friend of Katie gave a generous gift out of the surplus of their own adoption fund, which ended up being the exact amount of our first adoption agency fee. Random adoptive families gave generous donations to our fund simply to bless us. We would receive emails saying, "You don't know us, but we're excited to donate to your adoption." We had almost fifty volunteers help with our rummage sale and raised 20 percent of our support. There were parishioners and neighbors who would come to the checkout table with three books and a shirt, hand over a hundred-dollar bill, and say, "Keep the change." All of it was so overwhelming and beautiful. By March 2013, a mere nine months from the moment that we decided we needed to widen the circle, we were fully funded with hundreds of people now officially a part of our adoption journey.

Funny, it didn't feel at all painful at that point to open ourselves up and widen the circle. It's almost as if God designed us to live in ever widening circles.

CHAPTER 5

PREGNANT WAITING

I've quite obviously never been pregnant. I've lived through it with my wife, but I don't understand pregnancy and never truly will. I know that some women love pregnancy, claiming that they have never felt better in their lives. I know that other women hate pregnancy and after just one experience with it decide they never want to go through that again. There is no universal experience of pregnancy other than at some point pretty much every woman I've ever talked to (and husband or partner living alongside them) would admit that the waiting becomes heavy, whether waiting for the morning sickness of the first trimester to end or waiting for the due date to finally come in the third trimester. Most would also admit that the waiting is character building in one way or another.

I don't know what I expected in our adoption process, but I didn't expect it to mirror pregnancy in so many ways. The early days of deciding to adopt were thrilling and frightening. Telling our family, friends, and church that we were adopting was every bit as fun as revealing that we ourselves were expecting. The early months were filled with dreaming and preparations and enjoying others' excitement for us. The middle section was when things became real in our minds, echoing the second trimester of nesting and preparing. (Katie was always her happiest in the second trimester of pregnancies, and yes, she was so very happy in the middle section of the adoption process as well.) Nesting and preparing was quite different in the adoption process. Rather than lots of nursery prep (though there was some of that), we dove into the requisite paperwork. Katie was a machine. She was bound and determined not to waste a day of waiting because this approval or that paperwork wasn't completed. I've never seen her so organized and focused. Just as she walked with confidence in the second trimester of her pregnancies, she was simply glowing as she tackled the elongated checklist. Here's Katie's blog entry from November 2012:

> To stay encouraged, and to keep all you dear friends who are following in the loop, here is a list of what we have accomplished so far, and below that is a list of what we still need to do, including expenses, because we're trying to keep track. Your prayer can be that we can have our dossier finished and sent in to our agency, CCAI, by Thanksgiving! That's a month earlier than I had originally planned, but after working through the details I think we can do it! Pray for smooth sailing.
>
> Completed:
>
> 1. Paid first CCAI application fee and first program fee
>
> 2. Got Fingerprinted
>
> 3. Had physicals for home study
>
> 4. Completed 12 hours of online adoption training (+ criminal background check ×2)
>
> 5. Renewed/name changed both passports and passport photos
>
> 6. Shop2Adopt fundraiser raised ($6000). God is so GOOD!
>
> 7. Completed home study (!) and paid fee ($4300)

8. Collected: police reports (2), dossier physical exams/ blood work, marriage and birth certificates . Created: adoption petition, financial report, employment and non-employment verification forms

9. Had nine documents notarized and certified

10. Raised $17,945 through adopttogether.org. God is faithful!

We received (3) notarized copies of our home study in the mail last week. Hurray!

Still to do:

1. Grant request to AdoptTogether

2. Photocopy of birth certificates, passport photo page and marriage certificate

3. Send in completed I-800 A form to USCIS with supporting documents and fee to get our immigration approval

4. Send Lars's birth certificate to our courier in New York for authentication

5. Re-notarize employment verification (it was done incorrectly) tomorrow

6. Go back to Chicago to have home-study and employ-ment verification certified, then take ALL documents to the Chinese consulate to have authenticated

7. Print all family (×8) and couple photos (×3) for dossier

8. Make copies of passport photos (3 each)

9. Passport copies (2 each)

10. Grant Request to AdoptTogether for 2nd CCAI fee and CCCWA fee

11- SEND IN OUR DOSSIER to CCAI! Celebrate with the boys with dinner in Chinatown! Can't wait! If it happens by Thanksgiving, we could take the whole (crazy-idea) extended family downtown with us! HA! We'll see.

I share this list to give you a sense of the sheer amount of detailed work that goes into a Chinese adoption but also to dote a bit on my wife. When I read this checklist, I see a self-confidence and tenacity that I find remarkable. We were on our way. By Thanksgiving our dossier was indeed completed and sent off to China and by March 1 we were fully funded on AdoptTogether.

That's when the universal aspect of pregnancy hit us—the period of heavy waiting. Here's Katie from April 2013:

So, I finally started painting in the nursery. I have had a mental block about starting that project, feeling a bit lost lately in what I have dubbed "the silent period." The paperwork is done, the finances are raised (praise God), and there is nothing more for us to do. All is quiet . . . and we wait.

I finally admitted to my Tuesday morning women's study that it's getting hard. The waiting. We are officially a year in. Not long compared to some waiting adoptive parents. But it feels long. A pregnancy would have come to fruition in this amount of time. Our decision to adopt began with asking God to give us a name for our daughter, and he did one year ago this week (spoiler alert: we're keeping the name to ourselves until we get her referral picture).

We have been praying for our precious daughter by name for a year. She has existed in our hearts and minds for a year, and we're ready to meet her. I fell asleep a few nights ago thinking about having a spunky little girl with sweet black pigtails, running around our house. I know right where her crib will go in her room and I imagined what it will be like to walk in to see her sweet little face and messy hair when she wakes up from a nap. I imagine how very in-love I will feel, as I do with my boys. I'm so ready to know who this little one will be.

Pray us on. Pray for patience in the waiting, and then please pray that the waiting will not be long. That the phone call will come soon. Lars reminds me to pray for the call to come in God's good timing. And I do pray for this. But who knows, maybe that perfect timing will be this week, tomorrow even, so why not pray for that?

We did pray for that, but the pregnancy-like experience wore on, as did the "silent period." We waited for that call and then waited some more. We prayed and prayed, and yet nothing seemed to happen for a very long time. This very much mirrored the third trimester of our pregnancies, when I kept telling my wife that she was beautiful and glowing and that I didn't mind that she only had two pairs of pants that fit her. Now I was telling her that she was beautiful and glowing and that I didn't mind that we seemed to be floating through life in a perpetual state of waiting. I remember Katie getting a call from a Colorado area code (where our agency is located) and having it be a friend of a friend. She hung up the phone and cried and cried. I cried too. The waiting felt like it would never end. It's in times like these that you rest in hope, rest in a future that you cannot see, to get you through. Here's Katie from July 2013:

> In our first days as mother and father we received a special gift. It was a blue chair. Not just any chair but a nursery chair. One for rocking sleepy babies and nursing babies in the wee hours of the night. A wonderfully comfortable chair with a padded ottoman that silently glides back and forth lulling both parent and child to sleep.

Eventually it became a reading chair. My Book of First Words and Goodnight Moon and The Big Red Barn were read over and over to our sweet toddlers on their way to dreamland.

Both our boys enjoyed the blue chair, as did Lars and I. And then for a season much longer than we could have anticipated, the chair went unused. It was eventually taken apart and put into basement storage. I would think of the chair every time I went down to do the laundry and wonder when it would be used again. How long would it be?

Well I can happily say that the chair has found a new home and unexpected purpose. A few weeks back I finally finished painting the nursery walls a soft blue. And bit by bit the nursery is coming together. The crib was wiped down and set up. The dresser put into place. The bookshelf fixed. And then came the chair. The blue chair found a new home in the corner of the nursery.

We know we may be months away from welcoming our daughter to her new home. But the blue chair is ready and until we are able to rock our daughter in this sweet chair I have made a practice of sitting in it and praying for her. Lars has often come home to find me sitting in the blue chair praying for our daughter across the world. And although the nursery is not finished and there are curtains to be sewn, shelves to be put up, and details to finish, the reality of our daughter is feeling closer. Closer by way of a beautiful Asian baby-doll gifted from a dear friend, a precious Jade bracelet rediscovered after many years, and a sweet little sunsuit given by a sister.

We hope to learn of our daughter soon, the phone call could be any day. But until it comes I will enjoy the evening moments I spend in the blue chair praying for the little girl I will one day know. And my prayer over the last few months has been a simple one. I ask Jesus to hold her. By way of a nanny at the orphanage, or a foster parent, or simply as she lays in her little crib. Jesus hold her close, may she feel embraced by you.

How thankful I am to have my blue chair back again. And how thankful I am for its purpose in the waiting.

The waiting continued for several months. In that span we did get more calls from Colorado. Two of those calls were concerning little girls in China, proposed matches for us to look over. As much as we desired to have the waiting be over and to know what our daughter looked like, we had to decline these matches. At the outset of the paperwork is a medical checklist in tiny print, where you indicate which medical conditions you will or will not consider accepting in a child. It's an ethical minefield to even fill the form out. Obviously, if we gave birth to a child with any of these conditions, we would love them fully and completely and devote our lives to caring for them, so shouldn't we do the same for any adopted child? Thankfully, we had my father-in-law, Jim, who conveniently was a family-practice doctor, go through our medical check list with us and comfort us in the midst of what seemed like playing God. As we prayed about it, we felt led to bringing in a child with "special needs," but we didn't feel equipped or called for high levels of ongoing care that the more severe needs would require. We declined matches with two beautiful girls because of the severity of their needs. We wept and prayed that some other families felt led to bring these dear girls home as daughters. We trust that has happened.

So the wait continued. But not for long.

CHAPTER 6

THE MATCH

We read numerous books on Chinese adoption and there was a phrase that showed up in a lot of the memoirs we read. A 'Finding Place' is the place where an abandoned child, often a young girl, is discovered. This becomes important information because the government is obligated to run an add in the local papers indicating the child's 'finding place' and date so that parents have an opportunity to claim their child. To claim one of these children is exceedingly rare. Each time I read about a 'finding place' I was captured by the phrase. I was captured by the idea that, short of an accompanying note, this was the only known identity marker for so many children. They were defined by their 'finding place' and supplied later on with a name, an estimated birth date, an orphanage. But, for caring nannies and foster parents, the 'finding place' was a heavily weighted joy, the place where lives are changed in an instant.

Well, October 11 was a 'finding place', for both my daughter Lydia, and in many ways, for me as well.

Katie wrote on November 1, 2013:

On Friday, October 11, we learned we have a daughter in China!

This is how the wonderful news unfolded:

At 1:00 p.m. while driving with a new friend up to our mutual friend's house for a girls' weekend I got a call. Thankfully I was not driving. The call came after a few hours of driving. We were in Green Bay, WI and had just turned off on a detour. I saw the 303 area code and said to my new friend Kat, "This is our agency calling!" The call came after about a forty-five minute conversation about adoption including our story, as well as an adoption story in Kat's family, that ended by Kat saying, "So you could get a call anytime now, huh?"

"Yes," I replied, and fifteen minutes later the phone rang. It was Pam from the waiting child program at CCAI in Denver. She said, "I have a darling little girl I'd like to tell you about. Would you like to hear about her?" "Yes, yes!" I replied. She went on, "Her name is Wu DanQing and she is from Henan province. She was born April 10, 2012. She has a cleft palate and I think she is just precious!"

My mind was scrambling to do the math—April 10 to October 11—"So, she is eighteen months old right now," Pam continued. Eighteen months old, okay. I was trying to get my mind around this idea, she was a toddler, not a baby. Okay. "I just really want you and Lars to take a look at her file, so I'm going to send it to you, okay?" "Okay, yes. Thank you so much." Pam laughed at the nervous excitement in my voice and we said goodbye.

My mind continued to swirl. I was driving to the U.P. of Michigan. I wasn't with Lars. I wasn't with my boys. Would my cell service hold up so I could make the important calls I needed to make? And then the email appeared on my phone. (Praise God for the iPhone I had purchased just two months prior!) I opened the email and saw four pictures of little DanQing. There she was, this precious little girl who could be our daughter. Could it be? After I hung up, I told Kat I needed to pray. I cried and prayed that God would give wisdom to Lars and me to know if this was our daughter. I prayed the doctors would help us discern.

I called Lars. He was preparing to head up to the U.P. as well with a bustling van of junior highers to a Covenant camp just a short walk from where I was staying at our friends' house. But Lars would be hours behind me on the drive. He was nervous and thrilled. He immediately wanted me to call my dad to have him review the medical files, to help us decide.

I called my dad. He reviewed the file, even while I was on the phone. The medical information seemed so limited. She has congenital cleft palate. She has 10 teeth, her labs looked good. Her height and weight looked good. And that was it. No operative reports, because there had been no operations. She was a healthy little girl with a cleft palate. And then I asked, "Who else at Loyola should see her medical files?" My dad responded plainly, "Well, Kate, there's really nothing more here than a diagnosis. She looks healthy. She's not anemic and there's not really anything to ask about." He seemed amazed. I was amazed. (The simplicity of her medical condition amazed me because we had been presented with two other children's files over the spring and summer, who had such significant medical conditions that sadly we had to say no. This was so difficult for us and we began praying God would please not give us more than we could handle.) And here she was, little DanQing with a cleft palate. Something we could certainly help her with. Was this our daughter? I said, "Oh, my word. Dad I think this could be our daughter."

I called Lars and relayed the information. "Dad says her labs looks good. She's had all her immunizations. She has cleft palate, but there's no further information. I think she's healthy, she has a sweet full face so it looks like she's eating well." Lars paused and said, "What do you think?" I said, "I think this is our daughter, should I call Pam back and say yes?" Lars replied, "Oh, wow, this is our daughter."

And it was. Her name is Wu DanQing. Since April 2012, we have been praying for her by name. A name I prayed for before we started any adoption paperwork. Her name will be Lydia, Lars's great-grandmother's name.

I called Pam back and left her a message, saying, "Yes, we would like to adopt DanQing!" She called back minutes later, laughing and said, "Well was that the record fastest decision ever!?!" She was thrilled for us. I got off the phone and was still in shock. We had a daughter in China. She had been waiting for eighteen months. I was overcome. Thank you God for holding her in your care all these months. Amazing.

We texted family and made some calls. Everyone was thrilled. The rest of the car ride for me was sheer shock. I was still wrapping my head around the idea that our daughter was not an infant. She was walking, talking, eating real food. Her little write-up from the orphanage said she liked to play with balls, her favorite toy was a rocking horse, and she liked to pat the bows on her friends' shoes. It also said she did not like fuzzy toys and when she sees them she will cry. Hilarious! All we know of this little person is the information I was staring at on internet "paper." And I could not stop staring. Her picture was all I wanted to look at for the next few days. We arrived at my friend Courtney's house. I shared our news, showed the pictures, and was still in shock. The waiting was over. The seventeen-plus months of anticipation, over. She had a name and a face and a little personality. She was really out there somewhere, in the city of Xinyang in central China, on the other side of the world.

Lars got up to camp very late and came over the next morning. We hugged and looked at each other, still somehow unbelieving this could really be true. But it was and with each passing hour it was sinking in more. We prayed and thanked God through tears. The night before I had written our "Letter of Acceptance." Saying yes we want to adopt Wu DanQing. We plan to care for her medical needs and take care of her always. I noted how excited the boys were to have a sister. It was a sweet letter to write. Once the letter was received by the CCCWA in China it would be official and we could tell the world. It would be a couple days.

The weekend ended, and I went home to pick up the boys at my parents and stay the night. Lars arrived the next night after returning from his retreat. He came for dinner. We waited for Dad to arrive and then we told the boys. They knew they would get to learn their sister's name once we had a picture. So, we said we had something to make their already special weekend with Papa and Mormor and their cousins even more special. We told them they would get to learn their sister's name. We showed them her picture and shared the name and they were thrilled! Quinn even said, "I like that name!"

The next day we got word that the letter was received by the CCCWA. It was official, she was ours. The dream of a Chinese adoption I carried in my heart from so many years ago had come true.

Her name is Wu DanQing and she is our daughter, Lydia. God is so good.

CHAPTER 7

TRAVEL

Once we received our match our focus turned toward travel. Our agency, CCAI, had prepped us for what our Chinese travel would entail. Unlike some other countries that offer international adoption, China requires you to come to China and do all of your necessary paperwork at American consulates. Other countries, such as Guatemala, South Korea, Russia, or Somalia, require that you come and meet your child, then go home to finish paperwork, and wait for them to finish theirs, before traveling again to bring your child home. Korea used to arrange to have your child brought to the United States, so you meet your child at your own airport on US soil. China requires an extended stay only once.

CCAI uses this uniqueness to their advantage. They create an experience that is more than just adoption and paperwork. We knew that our trip to China would last up to three weeks and would include some touring in Beijing (hey if you're going that far, you might as well walk the Great Wall), time in the capital of your child's province waiting for paperwork, and ending in the southern city of Guangzhou to get a medical screening and the final okay from the US consulate. We also knew that whenever CCAI gave us approval to travel, the turnaround could be very quick. Both sets of our parents were on call and ready to stay home with the boys whenever we got notice that we could start packing our bags.

Here's a blog entry from Katie on New Year's Day 2014:

> After a whirlwind Christmas season that included all my family in town, multiple live-nativity Christmas Eve services, a great Christmas Day with family, a memorial service to celebrate the life of my Grandpa Peterson, my birthday, tea at the American Girl Doll store, and a lovely day at Covenant Harbor with friends, the email came through. It was THE email. The "you can go to China and bring home your daughter" email. I was in a store with some girlfriends and hadn't checked my phone in at least . . . five minutes. And then there it was on the screen: "CCAI—Travel Approvals Received—Please Read & Respond."

I stood in the store, trying to read as I was shaking! I cried (of course) and then called Lars back at camp. I woke him from a much needed post-holiday nap. He was thrilled! We saw there were two options for when to leave. Option one was January 8 and option two was January 15, depending on when they could schedule our consulate appt. Lars said, "Option 1!" I replied to CCAI's email, "Yes! Option 1!!!" That's literally all I wrote. So flustered.

We got back to camp and told the boys. We were all giddy! Albin said, "Mom, I feel a thing in my throat, like I want to laugh or cry or sumpin'. Maybe it's God working in my heart because I'm so excited about Lydia." Yep, Alby, it's called, "getting choked up." Too precious! We had a lovely night with the kids and our friends playing games and having great conversation. We got up the next morning, ate some breakfast, and got on the road back home. Just as we were headed to Walmart (to buy a changing table pad for Liddy) we got another email. This one said: "Consulate Appointment Confirmation."

AHHHHH! It was official. We would leave the 8th, meet Lydia on the 13th, have our consulate appointment on the 23rd and return home the 26th. Wow. This was really happening. We went into Walmart, I found the changing pad I wanted . . . and some bottles, and some cups, and spoons, and, and, and . . . Oh, my goodness! I responded to CCAI and our courier for Lars's visa, which we had to wait to submit because of his occupation. I called family and our travel agency.

The rest of the day was a flurry of phone calls and emails and finally in the late afternoon, the tickets were booked. This is happening! God is so good! We are coming, Lydia. Mommy and Daddy are coming!

And just like that, in a mere nine days, we bought our tickets, arranged our childcare, packed our bags, got coverage for my work at church, and prepared for the life changer.

On January 8, we boarded our fifteen-hour flight to Beijing with books in hand, movies loaded on the iPad, and an Ambien in each of our pockets. We decided that we would take the Ambien right away and sleep as long as we could. I'm not sure how it's physiologically possible, but the Ambien did absolutely nothing. We didn't sleep a wink. I guess adrenaline wins the day. If anything, the medicine made us a little slap happy. It was a flight full of intense nerves and equally intense laughter.

We landed in Beijing on January 9 in the evening. It was dark when we met our CCAI representatives and fellow adoptive parents at the hotel—five other parents in total from all over the United States: Tennessee, South Carolina, Florida, Kansas. We went to a noodle shop across the street for some dumplings to try and hold off sleep. We just kept saying to ourselves, "We're in China." It began to sink in that after a couple days of touring and resetting our clocks, we would be meeting our daughter.

Early that morning I awoke from a fitful sleep. I decided to write out my feelings:

We're all taught from a young age that there are no dumb questions, and as a lifelong learner, I believe that this is true. But I have, however, been asked this question no less than two dozen times in the last seventy-two hours: Are you ready? And my first thought was, Well that's a dumb question.

No, I'm not ready.

Sitting on our hotel room, looking out the window at the most other-worldly place I can think of, trying to grasp the magnitude of these moments in the life of our family—no, I'm not ready.

But to be honest it's not in my nature to be altogether ready. I'm a responder, an in-the-moment kind of guy. I'm not lazy, I prepare. But I'm not given to being detailed. It was Katie who packed most of our bags, who filed most of the paperwork, who thought through each moment. She is most certainly as ready as one of us could be.

My attempts at readiness are scattered and random in life. Oftentimes when I teach in a classroom setting, it's from an outline with just enough information to have good content and appropriate space to go down another path in the moment if necessary.

So if I'm not ready, what am I?

One of my favorite musical artists Teitur (Faroean artist born Teitur Lassen) recently released his fifth major album entitled *Story Music*, a collection of folksy, random stories set to rather dramatic and complex music scores. The first track has the following lyrics:

> Hopeful
>
> I'm always going to be hopeful
>
> Hopeful
>
> That's all I am

Since I first heard that track, these simple words have resonated with me. No, I'm not ready. But I'm hopeful. Maybe hopeful is all that I really am. I'm hopeful for holy moments halfway around the world. Hopeful for whatever reaction my new daughter has to Katie and I. Hopeful that, in the end, God will superintend all of the details, upset our life, and change us all when we are unaware and unready."

Hopeful, that's all I am.

CHAPTER 8

ADVENTURES

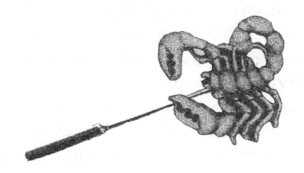

Our three days in Beijing were full-on tourism. I usually avoid looking like a tourist at all costs. When traveling in the US, I refuse to use a map publicly or eat at any place with a top rating from Yelp. When in Europe, I dress European and even practice phrases in another language so I can order food or ask for directions. But since I'm six foot two and I've got a red beard, in Beijing there was no place for pretense. So we went for it—maps, cameras, sneakers, fanny packs, bulky backpacks—we just owned it and it was great.

CCAI provided the full tourist experience. We spent a

morning and afternoon walking through Tiananmen Square and the seemingly endless Forbidden City. They gave us a true Hutong (Chinese alleyway) experience complete with a rickshaw ride and lunch in a Hutong home. We spent a day hiking the Great Wall of China and marveling at that feat of engineering. We walked through the Olympic Village from the 2008 Beijing Olympics. We convinced our guides to take us to an authentic tea ceremony to understand the art of Chinese tea. We ogled the locals in their public workout spaces, as the elderly were basically flash-mob jazzercising (yes, we stole a few excellent videos). And then there were the night markets. Here is my blog entry from January 10:

> Last night, we had the opportunity to stroll the night market just blocks from our hotel. This market consists of a long block of food vendors set up under canopies with steaming grills and hot pots and skewers of raw food waiting to be cooked. Oh sure, there is chicken, pork, Peking duck, fruit, and some sweets as well. But that's not really why you go to this night market. You go for the scorpions, snakes, eels, spiders, sea urchins, and unmentionable animal parts on a stick.
>
> Most of you know me as an adventurous eater with a deep respect for food and its role in culture. Over breakfast yesterday morning, I was asked by a fellow adoptive father, "So you're going to be a daring eater right?" I answered, "Absolutely." In my adult life, I've hardly ever

turned down food served to me, no matter how unappealing, and when visiting another culture the idea of eating at McDonalds makes me feel like an ugly American (though I'll bend on Starbucks). So when this gentlemen, Jon, ordered two scorpions on a stick popped one in his mouth and offered me the other I was conflicted. It is clear that much of the market is tourist driven—locals don't eat here. It's more novelty than anything else. And I was imagining how happy Katie would be if I was retching the next two days because I ate dirty street food. I declined. John ate the other. He's the man. White flag.

Trying new things is a value to me, a value that I desperately want to pass on to our children. An adventurous spirit is a beautiful thing. Well, some might say that this whole adoption is a crazy thing to try, something that will upset everything in life, something that has incredible unknowns, something that is so very foreign to the status quo of life. Well, they would be right, but Katie and I have parents who taught us adventure, abandon, and radical obedience to God's movement in their life. Katie's family sold their house and moved to Africa because God had put it on their heart. My parents took new moves and jobs without assurances of success because they felt led. So here we are, carrying on a legacy that we pray will define generations of Strombergs as well.

We are certainly trying something new, and in order to be fully present for this crazy adventure, I'll pass on the scorpion.

As the adventures in Beijing came to a close, the real adventure came into clearer focus. We packed our bags on January 11 to travel the next day to Zhengzhou, the capital city of Henan province, one step closer to welcoming our daughter into our arms and our lives. But we had one adventure left in Beijing.

With our bags packed, we invited one of our hosts to join us for dinner and take us to some place that locals ate, something that wasn't touristy (see, there is my image-consciousness poking through!). She took us to a massive shopping mall. On the fourth floor, in between a pharmacy and a department store, was a bustling hot pot restaurant with a network of counters with individual vestibules for boiling water. You are served meats, vegetables, and sauces ranging from mild to molten lava, and you cook your own food. It's a brilliant way to eat because it's time intensive and laborious, but it also gives you an opportunity to strive for the perfect bite while having lots of time to converse. Katie and I chatted with each other and our guide. The broth in our bowls grew spicier as we sipped away. I looked around and realized that we were the only obvious Westerners within sight. The smells, sights, sounds, and energy was

totally foreign to us, but I had a distinct feeling of deep in-
herent heart knowledge somehow.

The weight of this adventure began to feel less like a
backpack on our shoulders and more like an extra layer of
identity that we would be wearing for as long as we have
breath. Yes, these two days hence would change everything. They were clearly the defining days of our lives, the
enduring legacy of adventure that we would leave with our
kids. But in a hot pot shop in Beijing, the adventure became
delocalized. China was part of us now. No turning back.

CHAPTER 9

LABORING

On January 12, after finally having a night of semi-normal sleep, we took the two-hour flight from Beijing to the city of Zhengzhou (pronounced Jung-Joe), the capital of the Henan province. I had never heard of Zhengzhou before this journey, which is amazing because it's a massive city of ten million people. After Beijing it didn't feel so large, but it's wild to think that this unknown city dwarfs our home city of Chicago.

Our new hosts met us at the airport and moved us into a small bus to bring us to our centrally located hotel. I remember that bus ride being eerily quiet. As we drove through the grey, industrial, nondescript city, so very differ-

ent from the cosmopolitan Beijing, we were silently overcome by a sense of anxiety, excitement, and disquiet. I remember smiling as our hosts spoke with us about the day
ahead, trying to act normally but realizing that tourism was
finished. This was getting real. In one day's time, we would
be united with our daughter Lydia. Would she accept us?
Would she cry for days on end? Would she have physical,
emotional, or mental needs that we could never anticipate?
Were we really ready for this?

It struck me that I had felt this emotion before, once
acutely, and another time in part. Eight years ago we
packed a bag, took a picture, and got in the car so that Katie
could be induced to bring our first child into the world. The
emotions were the same: excitement, anxiety, disquiet—a
very strong sense that I wasn't ready for this but that there
was no turning back now. We would repeat this two years
later with our second child but with a bit less emotion. I remember feeling in both cases like I just wanted the labor to
be quick and painless (surprise: neither were). But in this
case I felt like I wanted more time to prepare, to pray, to
think this all through. We were looking at the finish line
around the bend, and I was slowing down with knots in my
stomach.

I looked around at the five other couples in our bus and
we were all quiet. Husbands were hugging their wives or
holding their hands. It was just like the calm before the
storm of going into labor. It was pre-labor, and much like

biological pre-labor, I was trying to console Katie while not letting on that I was freaking out inside. I was aware of my breathing in a new way, thinking through the checklist of things to do and wondering how to help keep us calm. It was like driving to the hospital all over again. We held hands while in labor, here we were holding hands again in a different sort of labor.

We arrived at the modest hotel used for adoptive families. Each room had two beds, a crib, and a rocking chair. This would be our home for the next eight days. Katie and I ventured out immediately to get some supplies at the local Walmart. Lest you think that this was a regular trip to a Western Walmart, allow me to paint you a different picture. This Walmart was six-stories tall. The first story was a meat and fish market that smelled exactly like you think it would smell. After walking through carcasses of beef and rows of less-than-fresh seafood, we made our way to the escalators and walked through rows and rows of housewares, dried herbs, and sundries. It was totally disorienting—just enough Western hemisphere to rope-a-dope you into feeling like you're home, and then you turn a corner and there is a fish tank full of live crabs or a whole section of mopeds.

The goal of this Walmart run was to stock up. For all we knew, Lydia might never want to leave the room or may not want to go in the room at all. We stocked up with treats for us and guessed at what treats she might be interested in. We had some information from the orphanage in Lydia's initial paperwork that gave us a sense of a dry, fluffy biscuit that she ate at her orphanage, so we located that and stocked up. We bought a massive bag of M&Ms because that always worked with the boys and we figured it was a universal treat, but we weren't sure.

We ate an early dinner at a local restaurant with the rest of our group. We were all tense and nervous but I remember there being chicken wings at the restaurant and thinking, "I'd like to take my daughter here and order these again." There was a group of Chinese businessmen who were desperately trying to buy drinks for the Americans, clearly in an effort to drink us under the table. None of us was even slightly tempted by these advances on this particular evening.

We were in our room by six o'clock that evening, at which point Katie went into nesting mode. With calm, prayerful, loving care she began to make our funny little room a home. She unpacked all the clothes, picking out Lydia's first outfit and laying it out on the dresser. Would they send her with extra clothes? She placed a blanket in the crib along with a stuffed animal and a makeshift bumper pad. What was her crib like in the orphanage? She placed shampoo and soap out by the tub for Lydia's first bath with us. Had she ever had a proper bath? She set books and toys out by the rocking chair and created a little space for Lydia to play. Did she even know what it meant to play? She had me pick out some calming music for whenever Lydia took her first nap in the room. Did she still take a nap? I was proud of Katie. It was really beautiful to watch her maternal instincts take over.

By nine o'clock the room was ready to go. We sat wordlessly, not ready for bed but too wound up to watch a dumb show or movie on our phones. We had prepared the best we could, but I think we were both aware that we had no idea whether or not we had prepared well enough. Katie suggested that we record a video for the boys back home, which we did. Then she had the brilliant idea of recording a video for Lydia of us speaking to her about our love for her and our excitement to have her be part of our family. We figured that it might be meaningful for her to be able to hear from us later on in life, especially if she faces the fundamental identity questions that most adoptive children face. I have never watched that video, so I'm not sure what we said. I'm saving that for a later date, so that whenever Lydia needs to hear these words, I hear them fresh as well.

Despite the pre-labor of sorts, we both slept some that evening. I woke up early and was immediately wide awake, which almost never happens. Katie was up early too, fitfully resting and willing the morning to come. I found the iPad and begin to write as Katie stirred:

"His mercies are new every morning, Great is Thy faithfulness! I say to myself, The Lord is my portion and therefore I will wait for him." Jeremiah utters these words in Lamentations in the midst of, well, his own raw and real lamentation as a reminder of the opportunities of each new day. It has been employed to many God fearers to impress the idea of second chances, God's faithfulness, and the invitation to a new start.

I'm so thankful for this daily promise of new beginnings and God's faithfulness in my life. But I'm thankful today for the particular mercies of special days. Days when you are fully aware that your life is about to fundamentally change.

Lydia DanQing is most certainly now in a van or on a train from Xinyang to Zhengzhou to meet two strangers who love her immediately and will necessarily change her life in every way. And she, in turn, will change ours forever.

It's a new day for all. The Lord is our portion.

CHAPTER 10

GOTCHA DAY

From Katie's blog entry, January 13, 2014:

We woke up around 7am. I had only slept off and on since 4. To be expected I suppose. We got ready for the day, had a nice breakfast, and gathered our belongings. We got on the bus and our CCAI representative shared all the "what to expect" information. It's normal for the child to be in shock, to cry. It's normal if the child bonds with one parent over the other for a while. It's normal for the child to have a glazed-over expression from all the commotion of the day. Whatever might happen, it's "normal."

This was helpful to hear again. As she talked, we passed by many tall city buildings, my stomach doing flip-flops. I sat squeezing Lars' hand, whispering, "This is happening." And then all of a sudden it was. One CCAI rep leaned over to tell the other something. And then she announced to the bus, "We just got word that the children from Xinyang have arrived—they are already here."

They are here?!? No time to think, to take in the room, to imagine the doors opening and our daughter being brought in. She was there waiting for us. She would be receiving us. It was all backward, and somehow it was perfect.

We pulled up to a grey government building, nothing remotely spectacular or fancy about it in any way. Katie was visibly shaking as we pulled in. I scrambled to grab my video camera and get it set and ready to go as we were being shooed off the bus. Our friend Jon, a fellow adoptive parent who along with his wife Andrea were waiting for their son to be brought to the building, offered to take a video of us meeting Lydia. I'm so thankful he did that because the video clip he took is one of our most cherished possessions. The video begins with Katie and me walking into the building. On the steps of the building, for a split second, Katie looks directly at the camera and smiles while letting out a visceral gasp of excitement. I don't know how to describe this small gesture and how much it means to me, but it encapsulates the enormity of the moment better than any word could. Every time I see this gasp, I get choked up and I love my wife even more.

We were barely in the door for three seconds when they said, "Lars and Katie Stromberg." That was it. Our moment. We turned to hear her nanny holding her say, "DanQing," and just like that she saw us and reached for me. It's true, it's on video. How and why she did that, I don't understand, except to say I had prayed for weeks that she would accept us, and she did. God is so faithful. Her hair smelled of jasmine, an unfamiliar, exotic scent. We stood there amazed at her. We were holding our daughter. This little stranger, stranger no more. It was so much to take in.

No doubt Lydia was in a fair amount of shock. Her expression was rather stoic, but still she seemed peaceful. No tears. No fussing. She looked rather exhausted, which I'm sure she was as she had arrived here after a two-hour-long train ride. As we walked the room, witnessing other families being formed, she clung to us quietly. She even rested her head on Lars's shoulder for a bit. Quiet and tender. I was grateful I did get a chance to ask her nanny some basic questions, like was she still on formula or regular milk. The answer was both/either. The nanny clearly liked Lydia. She was very smiley and said, "She's very outgoing. She eats well, she sleeps well, very happy, very active." I said a heartfelt, "Thank you. For caring for DanQing." And she responded with a sweet smile and said, "You're welcome, it is my job."

I tried my very best to be fully in the moment. I remember giving myself a pep talk at our wedding, willing myself to soak in the holy moment that would never be close to re-peated in this lifetime. I remember feeling like Spider-Man, standing in that beautiful Methodist church in Wheaton. Every sound and sight and smell—I was fully in the moment, my senses on overdrive. I was fully there with my emotions too. I had the same feeling in that drab government build-ing. I held my daughter. I smelled her hair. I watched Katie kiss her. I felt like I brought myself fully to those moments and they are firm in my mind, a truly holy moment.
Katie continues:

After about forty minutes, a few signatures, and official photos, we got back on the bus. Lydia was tired, she was wearing five layers of clothing and she was clearly warm. I couldn't wait to get her into the room and take off the layers to let her breathe. She fell asleep on the ride back, waking up when we got into the room. We laid her on the bed and began peeling off the layers. One puffy jacket, one pair of overalls, one pair of split-pants, two long sleeve shirts, socks, and shoes. We let her lay there for a few minutes in nothing but a fresh diaper and she seemed warm. She did have a low-grade fever so after a little medication we gave her a bottle. She had to work hard to take it because of her cleft palate, and even with the nipple cut to make it faster flowing it's clear it takes work for her to latch on to the bottle. But eventually she got it all down.

After her bottle, she was very playful. She liked the little cars we brought, and the finger-puppets and the books. She spent at least forty minutes carefully moving chee-rios between three different bowls. In most every way, she seems a very typical toddler. She likes things with hinges and she liked her bath. She loves to be held. Ly-dia's only tears came when we went to put her in her crib. She had slow, raspy sobs and we decided to just lay her on the bed beside me. I laid with her and she calmed. Eventually she stuck her thumb in her mouth and then, the best part, she would not let go of my hand. She grasped my fingers and slowly fell to sleep. It was heav-en.

My memories of this morning and afternoon with Lydia in the hotel room all run together. I remember it being a sweet time. Not a lot of words between Katie and me, just laughter, tears, and wonder at this beautiful little girl and her warm reception of us. It is often said that of all the senses, smell is the most vivid, the most emotionally charged. I'll always remember how Lydia smelled. I've smelled jasmine since but it's not quite the same smell. If I ever smell it again, I'll know it right away. It was the most exotic, foreign, lovely smell.

We joined the other adoptive couples for Italian dinner in the hotel restaurant. It was clear that every couple had experienced their own holy moments throughout the day. All six kids were having different experiences. Two of them had spent much of the day crying, one of them spent most of the first day in the hotel hallway not wanting to go into the room. We were a haggard and overwhelmed bunch. Lydia was very active during dinner. We realize now that she wasn't wound up for that dinner. It was simply the medication breaking through her fever and revealing the true Lydia. She was all over the place, fidgeting, playing with her food, making cute little noises, and even saying "more."

I hate to admit it, but I hadn't really entertained the idea of having a super active daughter. I figured that her first twenty months of life would put her in a shell of sorts, causing her to be docile and cautious. How foolish of me! From that dinner on, Lydia has been the sweetest bulldozer I've ever known: tough as nails, socially charged, hilariously funny, often way too loud for the room, and interested in everything.

This personality made itself further known back in the room that evening as she walked the room over and over, laughing, stumbling, humming away. She calmed down as the evening went along. As Katie wrote: "She did go to bed in the crib just fine after a nice slow bedtime routine, with bottle and book and singing. It was wonderful. Lars and I keep looking at each other, like, is she real, is this real? And ever so thankfully, it is."

We would spend the next day bonding with Lydia in the hotel room and on a trip to, you guessed it, Walmart, to get more of those biscuits that she was gobbling up. During that dreamy day, I sat down and wrote the following, which continues to ring true:

I can't escape the truth that I don't deserve this, and by "this," I mean everything I know. I was born of two great godly people, healthy, mentally well. So was my wife. Those four special people came from great godly people, and on and on it goes. There are certainly issues in our family past and present, but let's be perfectly honest, I don't deserve this. It's what we call grace.

I sit here writing not 6 feet away from a sleeping child who can't say the same. She only knew six days with her mother, and perhaps her father. She knew loving care givers in her orphanage, but they will fade from memory. In fact, I pray that the first 20 months of her life might fade from memory quickly because we don't know what the whole of her life has held thus far. She didn't deserve that. I think I'd call that injustice.

The beauty of adoption is that grace triumphs so severely and suddenly. We will call upon God's grace for Lydia as we continue to bond here in China, as we figure out bedtime routines and meals, as we bring her back to America to her loving brothers and a church full of grace, as we start to tackle medical issues, as we help her through a life with some significant questions. I trust that God, who is himself Grace, will answer us in his own way. But for all the grace still needed, I'm overjoyed to bask in grace right here and right now. Lydia is getting the love and care she deserves, which of course, none of us deserve.

Grace is the reality that we are experiencing here, and it's remarkable.

CHAPTER 11

STEPPING BACK

January 15, 2014, two days after the elation of meeting our daughter, was one of the strangest days of our lives. In the midst of so much hope and love and family, we found ourselves stepping back into the past.

The taxi picked us up at the hotel at 7:30 am to bring us to the train station. We boarded the bullet train with our lively, smiling daughter. I was pretty excited about this train ride. We cruised at three hundred kilometers per hour past cities and towns, farmlands, gray buildings, and dirt roads. The ride was as smooth as silk and it made us feel like we were traveling back in time, out of the developed Zhengzhou to the China of the past. We made our way to Xinyang, Lydia's hometown, another "small" city of about seven million.

Lydia bounced around from seat to seat on the train ride, jovial and playful. When we arrived in Xinyang however, she changed. As Katie posted the next day:

> We arrived at a government building where we needed to present some paperwork for Lydia's passport. It turns out they had already taken her passport picture, but we did have to take a family picture, not sure for what purpose. It was a quick visit. Lydia was not herself during the trip. She was sullen and sleepy, and it occurred to us that perhaps she felt unsure about reliving a trip she was on only two days prior. Same taxis, same train, same building. Who knows what babies can take in and understand. But, no doubt, she was rather quiet while in Xinyang.

It wasn't just Lydia's countenance that changed. Mine did too. Xinyang was grey and quiet. At first I thought it was a rainy, drab day, but when I realized that it wasn't actually raining, it occurred to me that this was merely smog, thick enough that you couldn't see past the third or fourth story of the buildings. I felt a smog in my mind and heart too, a heaviness that weighed me down. Katie continued:

> Then it was back into a taxi and off to her orphanage. We passed bridges and tall buildings. One building sign read, "Center for Breast Disease Care," another "Rural Credit Union." On we went, maybe twenty-five minutes and then

I read a familiar sign. It was the address I had written on the care package I sent a couple months ago. "Bao Si Bridge," I think. And we turned left and there it was. The orphanage, and for Lydia, also her "finding place"—the place she had been found by orphanage workers one day in early April 2012.

My mind was spinning as we pulled-up. Suddenly every person I had seen on the streets of Xinyang was important to Lydia's story. Any one of them could somehow be her relative, her sibling, her father, her mother. Any one of them could have been the one who brought her to the orphanage that day in early April. How desperate it feels to not know. How painful. I can invent stories in my head, but the truth is we will never know, and it would be unfair to Lydia for me to even guess. That reality is one she will have to work through on her own as she grows. The not knowing.

We had decided that we didn't want to confuse Lydia by bringing her back into the orphanage, so I opted to stay in the taxi with Lydia. She laid in my arms, awake but very still, somber maybe. I stared at the facade of the orphanage building, full of loathing and compassion all at once. Eventually she fell asleep. Katie wrote:

I got out of the car and was ushered past the entrance to a set of concrete ramps leading to the floor where Lydia lived. We passed by a floor where they housed a preschool. It looked well supplied with artwork on the walls. We got to Lydia's floor and I immediately recognized the outside hallway from the picture we were sent with her update. Where she stood in puffy red overalls. First we were shown the play-room. A ten-by-fifteen-foot room with foam play mats on the floor. There were cubbies but no toys, except for two plastic rocking horses (her development update said her favorite toy was a rocking horse). Were these the only toys? I am hopeful there were other toys elsewhere. The nannies were in the room holding babies. They were smiling, very sweet. Our CCAI representative said to one of the nannies that I had adopted DanQing. She smiled broadly, nodding.

While we were standing there, taking in the room, there was a commotion in the hall. A film crew was filming something for a local hair salon. They were suddenly in the room and filming another CCAI mother and me. Very strange.

Then it was on to see where DanQing had slept. We walked down the hall into a small room full of metal cribs —we counted twenty. The cribs were tied together end to end. Three solid rows with enough room to walk in the aisles between. I knew this would likely be the case—a room full of cribs—but somehow I had secretly wished for better.

The sleeping room I had visited in college was in a brand-new orphanage in Gejiu, China. It looked like a castle, with big open rooms, high ceilings, muraled walls and colorful play mats, and lots of sunlight. The cribs were blue plastic and all was clean.

I was overwhelmed as they showed me her crib. Had this really been her home just three nights ago? No blankets, just a bottom sheet. The babies were interested in us, some standing, some sitting, others crying with the commotion of visitors. I did ask to meet and have a picture with the nanny who primarily cared for Lydia. They went and found her for me. The other nannies whispered to one another and one finally told me how "young and beautiful" I was. Oh my. I smiled awkwardly. We commented to the one nanny who spoke English that we were amazed to see so many caregivers. She said, yes, and that all had been trained by Half-the-Sky, an organization that works with Chinese orphanages to teach child-care techniques and developmental programming, even starting preschools. Then in came Lydia's nanny, a woman with a sweet face. She seemed a bit annoyed to have her picture taken. Maybe it was bad form for me to ask. Or maybe she didn't want her day to be disrupted.

She was busy, I'm sure. I'm glad I asked because I want Lydia to have that picture. I did not get her name.

And that was it. The "tour" was over. A mere ten minutes and we were ushered out. They said it upsets the children's schedule to have visitors, which I totally understand. But there was no time for questions. No discussion with a nanny about DanQing or anything specific. I was going to ask about which brand of formula she had and how much at a feeding. But no time. On our way out we passed by other nannies with cups of rice and meat going in to feed the babies. We passed by a room with smaller babies. It had a vaporizer in it. We walked down a stairway and passed a woman carrying what looked like two gallons of rice in a metal bucket.

And then we were back in the courtyard. I did see a playground area, but we were told that little ones did not get to play there in the winter months. I don't imagine the workers have time or resources to dress little toddlers for outside play. Especially when there are two hundred children to care for in the orphanage. As I walked out I did take several pictures of the outside entrance, Lydia's "finding place." And then I got back in the taxi where Lars and Lydia had been waiting. And then I fell apart. Lydia was quietly resting on Lars's shoulder and I quietly sobbed.

I was overwhelmed by the "what would have been" verses the "what will be" for Lydia DanQing. I was a jumble of emotions I didn't/don't really know how to process. I was struck by so many things that made me sad. The small rooms, the shear amount of concrete and grey and cold. And the toys. Where were the toys? I told Lars, "I'm just holding out hope that the Half-The-Sky organization actually came and worked with Liddy at the orphanage. I would feel much better just knowing that."

We got back to the hotel, reviewed some paperwork with the CCAI reps, and then Jesus gave us a gift. Our rep Rita gave Lars a packet. The packet read, "Half the Sky Foundation: Child's Memory Book," starting July 9, 2012. And there it was. Lydia's history in pictures and development reports. Everything. Jesus is so kind, so gracious and loving to soothe my mother's heart with this gift. There were footprints and reports listed for every ten days. Pictures of her learning to sit up, to crawl, playing with TOYS, walking outside, holding flowers, playing with friends. I am overcome with all that we now know, or rather, all that we will know, because the entire report is in Chinese. But the moment I get home I will find my one Chinese friend and see if she can translate it for me. I may need to pay her—it's long. What gift for Lydia to have that memory book, some of the missing pieces to her history. And what a joy to think of sharing it with her when she begins to ask questions in a few years.

As Lars and I sat on the bed looking at the pictures together we experienced a strange combination of emotions. We were elated and then grieved all at the same time. Lars noted that we were looking at all that we have missed. We didn't get to see her learn to crawl. We don't know her first word. We were not there to hold her tiny hands as she learned to walk. But we rest in the peace that someone was. Nannies and the woman in the pictures with her. Someone was there to clap for her when she took her first steps, to say good job when she mastered a new skill. Someone cared, and that's what matters.

So it was indeed an overwhelming day. And I remain sad for the environment Lydia was in, for the amount of concrete and lack of stimuli, but here are some things I am thankful for. I am thankful that Lydia was well cared for—that there were many nannies at the Xinyang Orphanage. I am thankful there seemed to be adequate food—Lydia's thighs are a testament to that. And with our afternoon gift of Lydia's memory book, we are ever so thankful to know that Lydia had a good amount of intentional nurture from trained caregivers.

And now she is ours. Ours to teach and encourage and watch grow. We get to be her cheerleaders, her encouragers, her safe haven. And so much more. We get to tell her we love her, to hold her when she cries, to delight in her laughter, to introduce her to Jesus. She is ours. What gift, what blessing, what grace.

Every time I think of Xinyang I grieve. I love babies. I love holding them, feeding them, smelling the top of their heads, and watching them learn new things every day. To think that those sweet moments were spent in such a cold, hard place is a grief for me. I found myself praying that she would forget her experience at the orphanage altogether, that it would simply slip from her mind and wouldn't battle for her identity. Perhaps God has answered this prayer. But if he hasn't, I would hope that she remembers whatever love was there for her.

The truth is, no matter the degree of difficulty, it is an important practice to go back to places of pain. I think about the points of pain in my life, and though they pale in comparison to my daughter's, they are still real. The pain of lost friends in high school. The pain of getting dumped. The pain of a car crash where I should have died. The pain of rejection to graduate schools. The pain of miscarriage. These are real pains for me.

When I go back to these places of pain, either in my mind and heart or physically, I now have a visual. I'm just a little child in the back of a taxi, falling slowly asleep in my Father's arms. And no matter how gray it is outside, and how confused my heart is, I know I'm loved and cared for, and I know that I don't ever have to go to these places of pain alone.

CHAPTER 12

BONDING

I remember heading home from the hospital after the birth of our boys. In both instances, those first couple of days at home felt so important—holy days when we really got to know our boys and bond with them. There were lots of hugs and pictures and videos, but mostly a sweet, delicate dance of understanding this new kiddo and adjusting as a family. Remarkably, Lydia followed the same pattern.

On January 17, I wrote:

Today, as our hosts waited for our children's Chinese passports to arrive, we CCAI families had a free day to tour or rest before we head to Goungzhou tomorrow and start working on getting our daughter back home. Katie and I joined our Kansas City friends Jeff and Tracy on a day trip to the Shaolin Temple, a Kung-Fu mecca just a couple hours out of the city, and a beautiful opportunity to experience Chinese culture. We traded the heavier smog and concrete of the city for slightly less dense smog and rolling mountain peaks.

One thing you should know is that in Chinese culture it is perfectly acceptable to point and stare at others. We've experienced it ever since we've arrived. Some are inquisitive and want to try out a little broken English. Some follow you with kind eyes and warm smiles. Some simply stop their walking and stare at you like you're a panda at the zoo. We're raised in America to see this as exceedingly rude, a real etiquette faux pas, but it's a normalized practice on the streets of China.

And man, did I get some stares today. I spent the entirety of our four-hour tour with Lydia facing me in the Ergo baby carrier, laboring much of the day to keep her from pulling off her hat, kissing her on the cheek, and whispering little things about her brothers in her ears. The last hour, she slept on my shoulder. It was really great. But nearly every Chinese fellow tourist looked at me and laughed, smiled, stared, pointed. I typically would smile at them, say hello, and move on.

While this might be seen as rude to some, I had no problem with the pointing and staring at all. First, I'm sure for many locals, it is an exceedingly strange sight to see, and I can't blame others for noticing and being interested in why these white Westerners are carrying around a Chinese baby. But second, and most poignant, I don't mind the stares because, even after only three days, this is no longer strange to me. She is absolutely as much my child as Quinn and Alby are. She's not an interloper and truly never felt like one. She's my daughter and, though it may look strange to some both in China and when we return home, it's not the least bit strange to me.

So please, feel free to stare. She *is* remarkably beautiful.

On January 18, we moved to our final city before returning home, Guangzhou, where the US embassy is located and where final paperwork would be completed. Before getting on the plane, we received a "child update" from Lydia's orphanage, a summary of important information for us to know about our child from her caregivers. Katie blogged about it, directing her words toward our boys. As we were getting to know Lydia and bond with her, we wanted her brothers to have a jump start on that as well:

Boys, I hope this post will help you get to know your sister even before you meet her. The day we arrived in Zhengzhou, right after we hopped on the bus to our hotel, the CCAI representative, Rita, gave us an "update" on our children. It was helpful in learning a bit more about Lydia's daily routine, personality, etc. But here's what we have learned about Lydia in the four days we've been together.

Food Likes: Crackers, especially rice crackers. (Good thing our town has an Asian food market!), scrambled eggs, rice porridge, puffs (sweet potato especially), rice, M&M's, Pringles, bread, yogurt, noodles, Goldfish crackers, Multigrain Cheerios, baby food (we brought those little squeezy-food packets and she loves them).

Food Dislikes: Oatmeal, cold fruit, cold drinks, cold anything. If it's not lukewarm or warm, she doesn't want it. Unless it's a cracker.

Personality: The update report we got was right on. Lydia DanQing is lively. She is very active, maybe our most active kid yet. Hard to tell, because she has been exploring a whole new world of freedom in the last four days. So perhaps she will slow down eventually... perhaps. Lydia is sweet as pie. She is indeed very smiley and very affectionate. She loves, loves, loves to be held. She wants to be picked up all the time, and when you do, the look on her face is priceless. She is thrilled that someone is holding her. She is affectionate to almost anyone, which we will have to work on, per all the attachment books I read. Although, when a random woman tried to pick her up in a store today, she did lean back into Lars, rather than put her arms out, so that's progress. She laughs easily and loves to play. Lydia loves to share her food. She has fed me about as many Cheerios as she has fed herself. She offers toys to other children and pats smaller children on the head nicely. If she is over-tired, she gets feisty! But once she is asleep, she is out. She is also very clever. She knows where things belong and puts things away. She is great with fine-motor skills. She likes stacking cups and climbing and just today learned how to get down off the bed. Bummer. She also makes some awesome faces where she crinkles up her nose and she knows she is being funny. We can't wait to see how you boys make her laugh. It will be so fun!

What's new to Lydia?

- Stairs. She is doing pretty well, but she's a bit overconfident.

- Stroller riding. Sometimes she likes it, sometimes she hates it.

- Riding in cars. We learned that Lydia gets carsick. Yesterday on the way to the temple we visited, Lydia threw up everywhere. She was riding in the Ergo carrier facing backward and had done fine the day before. But after I handed her back to Lars for a change of scenery she promptly threw-up big-time. Soaked her outfit and Lars's pants. After riding the rest of the way in just my scarf (should there be more coming…) I did bring a change of clothes and we did okay. So, now that makes two of my three kids who get carsick. Good thing her car seat is up with yours, Quinn. You can show her how to look straight ahead to the road. Stay strong Albin.

- Not being bundled up in many layers every day. She has seemed to love being unencumbered by clothing.

- Being kissed so much. It's clear that she isn't sure what to make of all the kisses on the top of her head when she's in the Ergo carrier, and kisses in general. But how can we not?! Those chubby cheeks!

- Soft toys and blankets. She isn't sure what to do with the little dolly blanket and other blankets we have brought with us. They don't have blankets in the orphanage and certainly not individual little blankies. We'll see if she warms up to them.

- Going to sleep without nineteen other room-mates. The whole going-to-bed process is really hard for her. She fights it. She fusses and cries and tries to get you to play and rolls over and cries some more. She gets rather frantic. Honestly, boys, we don't know what to make of it. Rubbing her back does not help, nor does patting her back. We have tried walking with her, swaying, bouncing. Nothing is really working, but we will figure it out, Daddy and I. We have found that if we lay with her on the bed and hold her hand while pretending to be asleep, she will eventually calm. But it takes a lot of time, and she likes to grab your nose, which makes it hard to pretend you are sleeping. So, we will all need to be really patient as she learns to go to bed in her own room, eventually. I'm hoping we can teach her to like her crib and her room by spending good time in there with her. And Alby, Daddy and I thought of your nightly prayer for "no bad dreams" and we'd love for you to pray that for her too. Thanks, honey.

Hmm... what else? She loves other kids. She loves watching the two older boys, ages five and seven, on our trip. So, she will LOVE having two big brothers! We have shown her your videos, and she always tries to touch the screen when you sing to her. So sweet.

Daddy and I are really missing you boys. We are ready to be home and be a family. Lydia is a joy and we are so excited for you to get to know her. We know you will love her and she will love you! What fun it will be for you to have a little sister!

The bonding experience is a time-intensive process that requires a great deal of intentionality. I remember that we worked hard with every little stage for our boys. It seemed that we would get into a good rhythm of eating or sleeping and then something would shift or change in their lives and we would have to adjust. Well, our time in China with Lydia felt like that process at hyperspeed. Everyday there was something new to learn, and it wasn't all easy. Here are some of my reflections on day three in Guangzhou:

Good morning from Guangzhou. It's fifty-five degrees and sunny with only a little smog. Feels like San Francisco. It's great.

I've always taken pride in being a lifelong learner. I read a lot, I try to ask good questions, I invest in new hobbies and interests. It was drilled into me by a number of seminary professors (chiefly Paul Bramer) that one of the best things you bring to your congregation as a pastor is to continually be learning new things and sharing them in creative ways. I am committed to being a lifelong learner.

And now, one week into this new adventure of adoption, I'm realizing that there is quite a learning curve. With my own boys, we had a year-and-a-half runway to figure them out—their personalities, tendencies, how they slept, what they ate, when they needed comfort, when they needed loving discipline. And while things often change quickly, Katie and I feel like we know our boys so well that we can adjust to almost anything. If Quinn all of a sudden started waking up in the middle of the night, we'd find a solution. If Albin all of a sudden wasn't motivated by dessert, we'd figure something out (don't expect that one to change).

But Lydia is different. The runway is short. She's trying out language already. We haven't had the time to know her tendencies. We're just learning what is her real cry and what is simply fussing. All this while being mindful that her life is changing fundamentally, she's learning a foreign language, she's trying strange new foods, and she's slowly realizing that these two adults are indeed sticking around.

Our big challenge over the last few days was that all of sudden Lydia wouldn't eat. We had a stretch of about two days where she ate in total: one banana, less than a handful of Cheerios, and four bottles—this after watching her eat everything in sight for the first few days. Why? What changed? Does she have a stomachache? Was she just in shock the first few days? Did she realize that there is indeed enough food for her? Is she growing comfortable with us? Is she simply not hungry? We don't know. We're learning.

I realize that this will not change overnight. Katie and I will become lifelong learners of our own child, and she will bring new opportunities for us to be challenged in beautiful ways. And as Professor Bramer said, the best gift we can give our own children is to commit to being lifelong learners of who they are. It's a holy joy to do so.

And if you're wondering, Lydia finally chowed down Papa John's pizza last night and some soft fried bread this morning. We're learning!

Those days in Guangzhou were very important. We could sense that Lydia settled into the reality that we weren't leaving, that she was indeed our daughter. Amidst consulate trips, medical checkups, and visits to the hotel pool, we started to sense that she was becoming secure in our love for her. While those sweet moments were happening with our daughter, our interest in basic tourism was waning. Katie was completely over rice for every meal, and even I had to force myself to go exploring at some point each day. We began to reflect on the enormity of these weeks in China and the things that we had learned—both the anecdotal and the life altering. Here's a blog post from Katie on January 22:

In the two weeks we have been traveling, certain phrases have made their way into our everyday vocabulary. Two of the phrases were coined by a veteran adoptive family. This family is back to adopt their second daughter, and the last time they traveled with . . . drumroll please . . . seventeen other families. Oh my! Now that is a BIG group!

The first phrase is "80 percent" or "eh . . . about 80 percent." You speak this phrase in reference to something being almost, nearly, or kinda tasting like "home" or "American" or "the way you're used to it." And typically the phrase is said with a little shrug or twinkle in one's eye.

Here are some ways this phrase can be used:

"How was the burger from the hotel restaurant?"

"Eh, 80 percent."

"How did you like the grilled cheese?"

"About 80 percent."

"Good ketchup on the fries?"

"80."

We have been using this phrase a fair amount because at this point in the trip I just can't eat Chinese food for every meal. Just can't do it. The way I wouldn't eat a hamburger every day at home. Not that the food is bad, because it's not. It's very good, or most of it has been, but, man, are we all craving Western fare.

In truth our days revolve around entertaining the children and looking forward (or not) to the next meal. It's something to do. We are touring, napping, or eating when we're not doing something adoption-paperwork related, and the desire for Wester fare was the birth of the "80 percent" comment. The last time the veteran CCAI family was here they ordered grilled cheese sandwiches and felt they were good, but somehow, something was off, something was different. Maybe the cheese was only partially melted, or the cheese was only partially cheese, but no matter, something made the grilled cheese 20-percent not quite right. And boom, there it was: "80 percent." It's the perfect phrase. And it need not only apply to food. It can also be applied to street signs that when translated into English almost but don't quite make sense. Signs such as, "No Stepping," "No Funning," "No Noises," "No Matches." Yeah, 80 percent.

Now, we must share that two dining endeavors proved to be 100 percent there. One is good old McDonalds. But this is only 100 percent because it's not really food so you can't mess it up. True? True. The second is Starbucks. Totally 100 percent. Way to go, Starbucks.

The second phrase of the trip: "Survive and advance." The veterans shared this one right off the bat. They shared that when they had come to adopt their first daughter, she lived on pound cake for two weeks. The idea behind this phrase is, "Hey, you're in China, and you were just handed a baby, a tiny stranger. So just do what you need to do to get through the day. And if all they eat is pound cake, so be it." Survive and advance.

This has been very helpful to Lars and me. It was helpful when Lydia barfed all over herself and Lars. We cleaned it up, put her in new clothes, apologized to the van, looked at each other and said a silent, "Survive and advance" with our eyes. Or when she didn't eat for two days—spitting out food, throwing it on the floor, having a screaming fit in her highchair. We called it, left the beautiful breakfast buffet with hungry stomachs, walked by all the other babies happily eating, took a breath, looked at sweet, spent Lydia, and chose an attitude of "Survive and advance" as we headed toward the elevator. Or when she can't settle to bed, with huge crocodile tears streaming down her face. And she won't even reach for us because she has kind of blankly "gone inside" somewhere. We gently pick her up, let her cry into our shoulders, and after a LONG "eventually," she falls asleep. Another fit over, another day done. Survive and advance.

The last phrase is one Lars and I are using just between the two of us. And all parents know this well. But somehow, it's more poignant with this dear child in this scenario of family forming: "It's not about us, it's about her."

This phrase is us recognizing that this go around of parenting, and especially while on this trip, it's very important for us to remember it's not about us, it's about her. We may want her to buck up and eat the food we're presenting her. We may want her to stay in her stroller, or drink more water, or stop yelling, or sleep in her crib. But here's the thing. A few very short days ago, she was sleeping in a metal crib in a concrete room, with nineteen other babies vying for the nannies' attention as they cried. And, praise Jesus, that day is done. There will be time for order and correction and proper eating habits and appropriate behaviors and sleeping in cribs. But not now. Now is the time for extra patience and letting her lead the way. Now is the time for holding her little hand as she falls to sleep next to us on the bed. Now is the time for extra snacks and improper meals and whatever the heck she wants. We are building trust. We are proving ourselves present. We are becoming safe and familiar and constant. We are becoming something she has never known. We are becoming family.

We are here Lydia. And it's not about us, it's about you.

CHAPTER 13

COMING HOME

On our last afternoon in Guangzhou we realized that there was no way we were going to fit everything in our suitcases. We had picked up an inordinate number of souvenirs on our journey, most notable on Shamain Island, a Western-friendly urban island full of shops and stores. Katie had picked up the idea of purchasing sixteen gifts, one for every "gotcha day" through age eighteen—everything from squeaky shoes, to Chinese dolls, to pieces of jewelry. Realizing that we were well beyond capacity, we walked to a local strip mall to find a luggage store. We had about forty dollars-worth of Chinese Yuan left and really wanted to stay on budget as best we could. We purchased a suitcase for about the equivalent of twenty-two American dollars, the kind of suitcase that you pray and hope will come off the plane in one piece. As we walked out of the strip mall, black, junky suitcase in hand, it felt very real. We were indeed going home, and it couldn't come soon enough.

We were so excited to see our boys, to finally be home, but we also started to get nervous about the logistics of being home. We knew we had friends and family who were excited to meet Lydia, but we also had a church family who had been supportive of us from the beginning of our journey. They would want their time with Lydia too. We became concerned about how overwhelming this could be for Lydia. We desperately wanted to build upon the great bonding that we had already established. We talked about this with some of the other adoptive families and decided to write a blog post to make everyone back home aware of some of our concerns. It was not easy to write this one:

Well, we're officially done. We're done with the paperwork, visa in hand. Done packing, done shopping, done with Chinese Yuan money, and totally done with this trip mentally and emotionally. We're ready to come home in a way that is beyond words.

Lars here, our last night in Guangzhou. We head by van to Hong Kong tomorrow, stay one night, and then hop on a direct flight on Sunday morning— yes, the same Sunday morning we arrive in Chicago. The math makes my brain hurt too. We'll be on one of the longest flights in the world, direct to Chicago. Pray for sleep for Lydia.

So, with that in mind, we thought we might share some thoughts on our reentry plan. These feelings come from our experience with Liddy thus far, conversations with fellow adoptive parents, and a lot of reading on child-hood attachment. We do this because it's important to share our expectations with friends and family upon our return. Bringing this child into our family and community is so fundamentally different than bringing our newborn boys into our world. We think it's only fair to share a few important items to us. As we shared the other day, it's all about Lydia right now, and these requests are all in her best interests.

For the next several weeks, or perhaps months, unless we let you know otherwise, we need to be the only people to hold or care for Lydia. We request that you not pick her up or attempt to take her from our arms. Also, we need to handle feeding, diaper changing, clothing, etc. The reason for this is to ensure that Lydia understands who her parents are and that she bonds and attaches to us. God's design for the family has been disrupted for Lydia, and it will take some work for us to restore it.

So please don't be offended at home, church, or elsewhere when we don't pass Lydia around. Feel free to greet her warmly, speak to her, and give her a squeeze while she's in our arms. Lydia is not shy. In fact, our concern is that she is quite indiscriminate. She may well reach for you, and Katie and I will pull her back in our arms. Please understand that we trust and love you all. We haven't all of a sudden become germaphobes or anything like that. We're simply following good, sound wisdom. I am confident that it won't be long before Lydia is fully integrated into our family and community system and is attaching properly. Until then we'll be keeping her close and guarding her from confusion.

We hope you understand. Please don't be shy about knocking on the door if you're bringing anything over to the house (thanks for organizing meals, WOW!). We'd love to say hello for a few minutes, introduce Liddy if she's awake, and give you a hug for all the prayers and encouragement throughout this entire process. We're SUPER excited for you to meet Lydia, and it's hard for us to be so careful with her interactions, but thanks for understanding and supporting us as the process continues.

With this plan in place, we took a 4:00 a.m. van ride to Hong Kong. On any other day of my life, a free day in Hong

Kong would've been an exciting proposition, but this day, we couldn't even muster the emotional energy. Our hotel was attached to the airport and we never left. We roamed the halls, ate granola bars for dinner, repacked, killed time. We hardly slept before getting up and out to catch our morning flight. In the terminal was a McDonalds. We ate Egg McMuffins and realized that we spent our last eight dollars on breakfast. God provided to the very last penny and we stayed on budget.

One of the reasons that our budget was tight was that we decided to buy a seat for Lydia for our return flight home. We could've saved over a thousand dollars by surviving with her on our lap, but we knew that wasn't going to work well. It was hard to bite the bullet, but it was a decision that we were very thankful for. We got on the plane, put on our seatbelts, and set our eyes toward home. Here are Katie's musings after arrival:

We are home. (Insert "Hallelujah Chorus" here.)

The end of our journey was fairly smooth, or as smooth as it could be with a twenty-one-month-old on a plane for nearly fifteen hours. We left from Hong Kong ever so thankful for our last-minute decision to purchase a seat for Lydia, and there we sat, three ducks in a row, Lars and I so aware of all that was about to change. We would be a family of five. Lydia would be meeting her two brothers, her grandparents, her great-grandmother, and a dear friend of mommy's at the airport in a "mere" fifteen hours. Lydia DanQing Stromberg would become an American citizen once her feet touched the ground. So much was about to happen for Lydia, and there she sat in between Lars and me totally unaware. Beautiful.

The flight consisted of Lydia looking at a great board book, playing lengthy games of moving Cheerios between various cups, fitfully sleeping, shedding some tears, and taking one good, hour-and-a-half nap. It was a LONG flight. On a flight that long, watching the map screen on the seat back in front of you, go from fifteen to twelve to nine hours to destination gives no satisfaction. It's just a long time to be off the ground any way you slice it. Lydia did great. Honestly, she was awesome, and she didn't even kick the seat in front of her. Wow.

The only hiccup came during the landing when her stomach got the best of her and she threw-up a couple times. Poor kid. We were prepared with zip-lock bags and came away with no damage to us or her sweet little dress. But she arrived in America exhausted and pale. But hey, so did I, and I didn't even puke.

We got off the plane, gliding effortlessly through customs. And then it was time to present our "sealed brown envelope" to immigration. This was the final document of the adoption. We stood at the counter and handed the envelope to the officer. He looked at Lydia, said congratulations, and Lydia promptly threw-up . . . in my hands.

And there it was, a somehow appropriate response to the events of the day and a bumpy landing. A long plane ride, citizenship, meeting your family for the first time. I would throw up too.

We left immigration and walked through the doors. And there was the crew. Both sets of parents, my grandma Peterson, my dear friend Courtney with baby Joy in tow, and two sisters on FaceTime. It was wonderful. Lydia, fresh from a sick stomach, was a little apprehensive but did so well meeting her brothers for the first time. Lars and I hugged them first and then they met Lydia.

Watching the boys meet Lydia is something I'll never forget, mostly because it was a momentous occasion that seemed so very natural. It was everything that an airport reunion should be. Lydia cried the whole way home from the airport, and we realized that it was her first time in a car seat. There would be many firsts to follow.

When we arrived home, we were greeted by a large banner on our back steps with notes of love and encouragement from our church. They had stocked our fridge and decorated the house with Chinese New Year decorations. My mom had even ventured out to our local Asian market to get Lydia's favorite snacks that she had seen on photos from our blog. Our family and church had taken our words to heart, overwhelming Katie and me with love but not all showing up at the house and overwhelming Lydia with their presence.

Katie continued:

The rest of the day was spent letting Lydia explore the house. To think, she had never been in a house. Never climbed stairs. Never seen a fridge, a dishwasher, a fireplace. She walked around, content to look and wander, occasionally making sure Lars and I were close by.

Lydia seemed content and surely tired as she played and explored the house. But truly, it just felt good and even somehow "normal" to see her walking around and playing with blocks and her brothers' matchbox cars. Like, of course, it's just as it should be. And I know Jesus agrees. After all, this was the story he chose to rewrite for her life. This was his idea, not ours. This is his working faithfulness. And he was smiling yesterday. Smiling because all is as it should be. Lydia was rocked to sleep in the blue chair, she ate dinner with her brothers and grandparents, she has clean clothes and a warm house and toys to play with, she is safe and treasured and so deeply, deeply loved.

And as I think on the last twenty-four hours, my eyes fill with tears because Jesus is smiling on little Lydia Dan-Qing Stromberg who is finally and forever home.

CHAPTER 14

BECOMING WHOLE

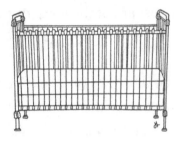

We knew that we would be facing surgery after returning home for Lydia's cleft palate and we had been advised that we should consider having it completed as soon as possible. The sooner the surgery, the sooner we could assess the scope of her medical needs and get her the help she needed, especially the speech services that she would require. We contacted the cleft team at the University of Chicago and had a consultation scheduled within a couple weeks of being home. And no, it's not lost on me that we happen to live in a city that has hospitals with cleft teams. It's truly remarkable realizing that we could live any-where in the Midwest and be traveling to Chicago for this team, and yet here we are.

On February 20 we had our big doctor appointment for Lydia—her first evaluation by the cleft team to determine what exactly was going on in that little mouth of hers. It was a great appointment, and her first surgery was set for two weeks later, March 5.

Here's Katie's post about the surgery and Lydia's re-covery:

We got into the University of Chicago on a snowy morn-ing at 7:15 a.m. We met the anesthesiologists and other doctors who would be working on her in surgery. The primary surgeon is a wonderful man who has great bed-side manner and has clearly done this particular surgery many times. What a blessing. We got Liddy all dressed in her little "gown," gave Daddy ("ga-ga") a big smooch, and off she went with the sweet anesthesiologist resident. The doctor was extra smiley and put Lydia at ease—that and we let her bring the tube of Chapstick and Aquaphor she found in my purse into surgery.

Then we waited. We walked down the hall and got on the elevator. I had some tears. Just nerves, I guess. We ate some breakfast downstairs and came back up to contin-ue to wait. We texted and read. Lars took a cat nap and then we got a call from the surgeons about an hour and a half later saying the stage one cleft repair was complete and now the ear tubes would be put in. Great news! The surgeon came out and said the surgery went well. I asked to see pictures and he showed me a picture on his camera. They made little incisions in her inner cheek to allow the uvula to come together in the back of her throat. Pretty fascinating to see. We shook the surgeon's hand, said a big thank you, and a wash of relief came over me. We were close to being finished. I had not been away from Lydia for this long in her waking hours and it felt strange.

It was at this point that I had a revelation about recovery. I asked the doctor if we could please not put her into a crib for recovery. I knew she would freak out and honestly anyone might. The part of the crib without bars is covered in plastic, and frankly it's exactly like a cage. Forty-five minutes later we were called again and told they would be moving her to recovery. We followed and found our little munchkin laying there peacefully in her bed, still very much asleep.

She was hooked up to lots of monitors. But her oxygen looked good and we waited. It was close to forty-five minutes before she started to stir, at which point I was able to get into the bed and hold her. Perfect. She was groggy for a very long time but rested peacefully in my arms. We had to wait for a bed to open upstairs for nearly two hours, but when it finally did, we were moved there quickly and were relieved to have some privacy.

The nursing staff was wonderful and Lydia hardly fussed. It was now 2:45 and Lars and I ate some lunch. Lydia woke and fussed a bit on and off all evening and through the night, but likely from discomfort, not pain. She was medicated and all in all she was a champ! Nurses came in throughout the night to check various monitors and see how she was doing, and mainly she stayed sleepy. She did wake at 3:00 a.m. and wanted to drink, which was awesome. One step closer to getting to go home! And thank goodness she did so well and I didn't need much help because poor Lars was out of commission with some form of food poisoning from the Au Bon Pan downstairs. Bummer.

The next morning, Lydia was more awake, looking at books and wanting to eat, so she ate some squeezy baby foods. Then the doctor checked in and after a bit more waiting, we got to leave around 1:00 p.m. Hurray! All in all, a really good experience, as hospital stays go. Funny thing, a couple nurses commented on swelling in her face, to which I replied, nope those are just her cheeks! Seriously she wasn't swollen. LOVE those cheeks!

Lydia's recovery at home has included all pureed foods, which she's sick of, and wearing little arm stabilizers that don't allow her to bend her elbows and reach her mouth.

Kind of sad to see, but she manages to play just fine with robot-like arms. Her next surgery will be in the fall, and we hope that surgery will close the opening and allow her to focus on learning to talk with the help of speech therapy. For now, we are just happy that we have one surgery behind us. One step closer to a repaired cleft.

And, to think, for seventeen of the seventeen and a half months we waited for Lydia, cleft palate was not a medical condition we had said yes to. It was not on our list—it seemed too daunting. But God knew better and he gave us a change of heart at the perfect time. Lydia's cleft palate, her "special need" is the very thing that brought us together. So, with each surgery I will remain grateful for God's good timing, for his good plan for Lydia's life, and for the "special need" that brought Lydia into our lives.

■

We were tired in the following weeks and we rested, just as if we had brought a newborn home. We were severely jet-lagged, but we were emotionally spent too. The freezer full of lasagna and casseroles was a life saver because we didn't have much energy to offer our kids dinner every night. I was adjusting back to work, Katie was settling back into school rhythm, and Lydia was adjusting to her new reality. And exactly like having a newborn, all we wanted to do was sleep, and the only thing Lydia didn't want to do was sleep. Here's Katie from April 2014:

The last ten weeks have been full as we have become a family of five. It's a whole new dynamic. And we are quickly finding a new normal. And, honestly, I'm amazed to say the only real bump in the road has been sleep. While in China we had some sleep struggles, and after an initial two weeks at home of what I might term "happy shock" and decent sleep, Lydia wised up. She realized that we are here to stay. Day after day, we were not leaving. And so she has been bonding, like all-in, really tight, don't-leave-me-ever bonding. This is great. Except for the fact that she only wanted to sleep in the blue chair with me holding her for hours at a time. Or in our bed, which was not working for either Lars or me.

Then came surgery. She did great. She was a champ, and truly we hoped that perhaps how very tired she was post-surgery or the medications she was on would send her to peaceful rest in her crib. Not so.

Then Lars finally said the words I didn't want to hear. "Kate, I think it's the crib." My heart sank, because I knew he was right. It was the crib. Lydia had spent the first twenty-one months of her life mostly confined to her crib. It was her playpen, it was where she ate (we saw this at the orphanage), slept, and probably sat for hours every day. But for me, her crib meant one thing. It meant she was a baby.

I had sat in my blue chair for months dreaming of and praying for the baby girl who would love that crib, who I would peacefully lay down to sleep in that crib, that sweet crib gifted to us from a church family when Quinn was first born. The bumper, my only splurge, that I had carefully chosen and based the whole room around. The eighteen-dollar vintage Swedish tablecloth I had turned into a crib skirt after hours of searching on Etsy. I thought she would love it.

I roll my eyes at myself when I think of how attached I was to the whole idea of that crib, but when you don't get to have a pregnancy in anticipation of a child, you put your maternal energies into cribs and nursery colors and honestly anything that makes you feel like you are pre-paring for something BIG.

So taking it down meant all those hopes of her loving it were not to be. But more so it meant I had to be honest with myself and admit that although Lydia seems in so many ways a baby, in truth, she is a toddler. I had to let go of my desire to "hold on" to the crib, since it was clear it would not help Lydia sleep peacefully through the night. And I had to quickly work through my sadness over each step we had to take away from her "baby-dom." A sweet "baby-dom" that, sadly, we had missed out on. We already had to take away her bottle prior to surgery, and now the crib too?

But the truth remained that Lydia had decided she was done with cribs and no amount of Jenny Lind spindles, or Pottery Barn bumpers, or soft blankets would make her like it. She was done. So, just as Lars knew I would, I had a "moment." I sat down in the blue chair, had some tears, took a breath, and watched as Lars dismantled the crib. He even left it in the boys' room for a couple days, in case I should want to put it back up. But I knew it was down for good.

The next day, we decided to go for it. I went mattress shopping and we brought up from the basement the beautiful bed a sweet neighbor had gifted us for Lydia. It was perfect. And Lydia loved it immediately. Again I had tears—this time happy ones.

We then spent about a week taking turns sleeping with Lydia in her bed. She slept; we didn't so much. We began a very deliberate bedtime routine. Same book (*The Big Red Barn*), same CD (*Hidden in My Heart: A Lullaby Journey through Scripture*), prayers, kisses. And the very first night she fell asleep peacefully, no tears, no fussing.

And because God is God and he wants to show me over and over that he does indeed care about the details of

my life, I watched as Lydia drifted to sleep to the following lyrics. "I will never leave you, nor forsake you. Know
that I am with you. You will never be alone."

And that is God's word for Lydia. His truth and my prayer.
She will never be alone. This idea struck me to the core.
This is one of God's most incredible promises in Scripture. To never leave us orphans. How grateful I am to live
into this truth daily. God is with me. I can know him. And
because of this truth, I can rest. And so too can Lydia.
She can rest knowing she is not alone.

The day after the big-girl bed went up, Lars preached a
sermon. It was about this truth from Scripture and about
Lydia. After a couple weeks of sleeping with Lydia, we
moved to sitting in the blue chair until she fell asleep and
then quietly slipping out. And then just three weeks ago,
Lars decided to try what had worked with the boys. He
said goodnight and left the room. She cried. He came
back in, said, "Put your head on your pillow, honey.
Goodnight, love you, I'll be here in the morning." He left,
she cried. He did this for an hour. And then she finally put
her head on her pillow and went to sleep.

And that was it. She sleeps. And the key words for her
were "love you, I'll be here in the morning." I have actually
watched her body relax as I speak those words. She is
believing those words to be true. She is resting.

Three months ago today, Lydia walked into my arms and went from orphan to beloved daughter. And by God's grace she is resting in our love and in knowing that we will be there in the morning. She will never be alone. How good God is to give her (and us) that awesome promise.

CHAPTER 15

THE STORY UNFOLDS

L ydia's story deserves multiple volumes, far more than can be written here. As the months and years have unfolded, so has Lydia's story, and it has become richer and more layered in time. There are many chapters of her story that didn't make it into this volume. There should be a chapter on her many firsts—her first time swimming in a lake, or running in grass, or going to the movies, or meeting her aunts and uncles and cousins, or ice skating, or walking through Chinatown, or eating Swedish meatballs.

There should be a chapter on the answered prayers that we observed. Katie started praying whenever she saw a clock land at 11:11, morning or evening. She still frequently will turn to me when I'm half asleep and say, "11:11," and then begin fervently praying for Lydia's mother and father in China, that they would know that Lydia is safe and loved and that they would come to know the love of God in their lives. We will likely never meet them, or know if those prayers are being answered, but we keep praying every time we see 11:11.

There should be a chapter on the miracle of cleft-palate repairs. The process itself is mind blowing: to start with a gaping hole on the roof of Lydia's mouth, straight into her nasal cavity, and to end nine months later with a perfectly pink, fleshy palate. You would never know that there was ever a medical problem that would ultimately designate Lydia as a "special needs" child, a designation that would unite us as a family.

There should be a chapter on speech therapy. We were amazed at the various speech therapists who entered into Lydia's life, training her to speak with her newly constructed palate. We have had a procession of loving and caring speech therapists, both in our home and in our school, who have worked tirelessly and patiently with Lydia. It's because of their faithfulness that Lydia entered kindergarten without any speech intervention—a truly remarkable feat.

There should be a chapter on her earliest questions about her biological mom and nannies in China, her questions about where she is from and her pride in anything Chinese. We know that the toughest questions are still to come, but her sweet investigation of her early childhood has been touching and often heartbreaking. Her story will follow her going forward and we hope that we'll know when to answer as best we can and know when to simply cry with her at what we do not know.

Yes, there are many chapters that have been left on the table. So where to end a story that still feels like it's just beginning? Well, in a hopeful place. From Katie on January 2018:

Four years ago today, Lydia walked into our arms on a cold day in an official government building in Zhengzhou, China. It was truly one of the best days of my life. A day of tiny miracles all wrapped up in this little girl. And as is God's way, He was at work back home in another mother's heart, working a miracle that would only come to fruition three years later. So, as I am reflecting on the miracle of Lydia today, my heart and mind are extra full because we have been witness to another adoption "miracle on 4th Street" and that story needs to be told.

International adoption is no small thing. It requires incredible resources and waiting and patience and trust. Trust most of all. But it all begins with a desire, and it's not merely a desire to expand your family—that feels somehow too simple. Choosing to adopt from China means you are open to a child from another culture, a child with potentially complicated health issues, tons of paperwork, waiting, more waiting. International adoption is not the easiest road and the parents I know who decide to pursue it definitely feel a pull, a heart tug, even a sense of calling to it. Such was the case with my friend Anna.

The day after we got off the plane with Lydia back in late January 2014, our doorbell rang. There stood our neighbor with a welcome gift for Lydia. I invited her in. Lydia was standing there with me and she offered us her gift, a sweet stuffed pink and white giraffe. She welcomed Lydia and then got choked up standing in our entry. I didn't really know her all that well and I didn't know what was happening for her until she said through teary eyes, "We have been following your blog and your journey with Lydia and we've always thought about adopting from China and we're going to do it." In my fresh-off-the-plane-from-China-with-a-toddler stupor, I'm not sure exactly what I said. I was stunned. Oh, my word. She was our neighbor across the street. Of all the people in the world to feel the pull, the same heart desire, it was my sweet neighbor? Just wow.

What has transpired over the last four years on 4th Street has been evidence that God is ever so real. Like undeniably real. This dear family across the street decided to go with our same agency, and with a preschooler and a baby at home they began the process to adopt a little girl. Anna and her family attend our church, and over the past four years we have been in each other's homes for book studies and Bible studies together. We have prayed together and cried together when the waiting seemed too much to bear. This adoption journey has turned us from neighbors into precious friends.

And then on May 31st of this past year, when it seemed impossible to wait any longer, the call came from the agency with news of a little girl in a group foster home that needed a family. Her name would be Savannah, and we had been praying for her by name for well over three years. As I stood with Anna looking at pictures of this precious little girl with an already repaired cleft lip and palate, I was overcome again. How incredibly gracious of God to put us in each other's lives in this season. Three plus years is a long time to hope and pray and wait. But to know others are hoping and praying and waiting with you is everything.

Four years ago Anna watched out her window as we pulled into the church parking adjacent to our house bringing Lydia home from the airport. And this August I watched out my front window as Anna and family left for the airport to go meet Savannah. As I sat watching them pack up the car, I just wept at God's faithfulness. And I'm weeping even now as I write. Two miracles have occurred on 4th Street. There are two less orphans in the world, there are two families now complete.

How can we ever know the story God is writing for our lives? How can we fathom the intricacy of his plans? How could he choose not one but two families in the same town, on the same street, to be forever changed by two little girls born half a world away. Just how?

Yesterday I got to watch Savannah for a bit while Anna was at a meeting. We played with babies and rolled balls and read books and it's still totally surreal to have this precious little gem living across the street. And somehow it feels like Lydia and Savannah have always been with us. But I pray I never stop being amazed at the way God worked to weave our stories together. I will never forget that day back in January 2014 when Anna rang our doorbell and shared how Lydia's story had spurred them on to make a decision to adopt. I remember thinking how insane it was that Lydia had hardly been on American soil for twenty-four hours and God's purposes for her life and story were already being worked out. Lydia doesn't understand all of this—she's five. But someday she will see Savannah's adoption as a part of her story. And we will marvel at it together.

For now, we are ever so grateful to share this China adoption bond with these dear friends. While she was in China, Anna and I texted daily about all the emotions and the ups and downs of bonding and forming as a family. What a gift that we will have one another to lean on as the girls grow, as they have questions, as we need to process with someone who understands. And our precious daughters will have one another, someone in a family like theirs. Someone who understands what it's like to be them, in a family formed by adoption.

So, today as we celebrate Lydia with her requests for presents, Chinese food, and *Dancing with the Stars* reruns, we are surely celebrating God's good work in bringing Lydia into our family, but we are also celebrating Savannah and how God works in ways we could never imagine. Praise God for his miracles on 4th Street.

Yes, the story continues to unfold and I am confident that God will continue to surprise us along the way. We'll continue to witness miracles in places both mundane and sublime. The lesson in this unfolding story is that God is at work in ways that we could never comprehend. That's as true for you right now as it has been throughout our journey with Lydia. He brought together two stories of brokenness, of a couple grieving and a child half way around the world. In Jesus, the lost are found. I know this because I was lost, and through God's grace named Lydia, I've been found. For that I'm thankful.

AFTERWARD
(FROM KATIE)

The call to adoption was in the making for many years, and we are confident that we have been led each step of the way by God who has great purpose and plans for our family.

Here is what we like to call our, **'Timeline to China'.**

26 years ago (1994) I traveled with my mother to Ukraine on a missions trip to work at a summer camp for orphans. And my heart began to stir.

25 years ago my mother accompanied a dear friend to China as she adopted a baby girl. And my heart continued to stir.

24 years ago my dad encouraged patients of his and friends of our family to consider a Chinese adoption. They did. I babysat this precious little girl and over the course of high school began to learn of her journey from orphan to beloved daughter. And my heart was moved by the plight of orphan girls in China.

21 years ago I began studies at Bethel University. I studied China's one child policy and researched the subject for my Sociology major. I began to feel a heart tug to consider Chinese adoption someday.

20 years ago (2000) I had opportunity to visit a state run orphanage in GeJiu, China, while on a mission trip. I held the orphan babies. I prayed over them and while on that trip God confirmed in my heart that I would one day adopt a little girl from China.

19 years ago, I shared my adoption dream with my college boyfriend, now husband, Lars. He readily agreed that one day we would pursue this dream.

17 years ago (2003) I married my love Lars Stromberg. That same year my older sister Emily was hired at a Chinese adoption agency outside of Denver. An agency called CCAI with a Christian vision to find forever families for the orphans of China.

16 years ago Lars and I learned that we did not meet the rigorous qualifications for Chinese adoption. And the China dream was "put-on-the-shelf" for a season.

14 years ago (2006) we welcomed our first child. A little boy, Quinten James.

12 years ago we welcomed our second son, Albin Robert.

10 years ago we began trying for baby number three. We became pregnant three times in two years. But lost all three pregnancies to miscarriage. Lars and I were deeply grieved by our losses. And then I read a book that changed everything.

8 years ago (Feb. 2012) Five weeks into our most recent pregnancy, I read a book called <u>Choosing to See</u>, about the journey of Mary Beth Chapman into motherhood, Chinese adoption, and the grief of losing a child. As I turned the pages, my heart was deeply stirred again for the orphan girls of China and for the calling to adopt.

April 2012 our pregnancy ended in miscarriage. But, our grief turned to hope as our thoughts turned to the dream of a little girl in China.

May of 2012 we discovered we now meet all the qualifications to adopt from China. Lars and I prayed. We talked. We prayed some more, and decided the time had come to pursue our China dream.

Late May of 2012 with the acceptance of our adoption application, we began the journey to our little girl in China. It was a long journey but we knew the God who stirred my heart so many years ago, is the same God who aligned our hearts to the dream, and the same loving Father who would provide each step of the way. And oh, how he has.

7 Years ago, in mid October we got a call from our adoption agency with a 'match', a little girl, named Wu DanQing.

6 years ago on a cold January morning in Zhengzhou, China, Lydia DanQing Stromberg walked into our arms and became our beloved daughter. God is good.